About the Author

Bob Gerberg has a BA degree from Colgate University and an MBA degree from the University of Pittsburgh. After several years as an Air Force officer, he had a successful career with major food companies, including positions as a Vice President of Marketing Services and Assistant to the Chairman of a Fortune 500 company. Active in the career field for more than a decade, he has authored dozens of publications and cassettes on career transition.

Princeton/Masters is a high-level outplacement consulting firm with offices and associates in major cities. The firm's specialty is in managing private marketing campaigns for people seeking new positions.

The Professional Job Changing System. Copyright ©1996 by Robert J. Gerberg. Second edition publishing date September 1, 1996. All Rights Reserved. Printed in the United States of America. No part of this book may be used or reproduced in any manner whatsoever, except in the case of brief quotations in articles and reviews.

Library of Congress Catalog Card Number 96-069170
ISBN 1-882885-09-0 (cloth)

Books by Princeton/Masters Press are available at quantity discounts. For information, write: Princeton/Masters Press Inc., 7951 E. Maplewood, Suite 333, Englewood, CO 80111 or call 800-772-4446.

The Professional Job Changing System

An Easier Way to Find the Right New Job

A Princeton/Masters Publication
By Bob Gerberg

Contents

1
How to do a Professional Job Search

A recent cover of **Time Magazine** *included the following: "About finding the great American job... the rules of the game have changed forever." The problem for most people is that they simply don't take a professional approach to job hunting. Here's an overview of how to make your career search easier, faster, and far more predictable.*

Most people start by preparing a "tombstone resume" that typically says, "Here lies John Doe, went to these schools, had these jobs." Then, once they get their resumes together, they just scatter them as they answer some ads or visit a few recruiters or personal contacts. Some send out mass mailings using poor materials, the wrong lists, and the wrong techniques. In short, their approach is haphazard, expensive, full of dead-end leads, and they end up job hunting for a long, long time.

In a recent article, *Business Week* also said executives who lost jobs should plan on 18 months of unemployment, and the U.S. Labor Department has been quoted as saying it takes a year or more. One of the reasons, however, is that as important as contacts and networking can be, most people rely far too much on these methods for uncovering new situations. This is clearly underscored by the data on the following page.

When they land a position, the way in which their "traditional methods" enable them to find their positions may surprise you:

- 60% from existing contacts and direct referrals
- 22% from networking efforts (indirect referrals)
- 9% through contact with recruiters
- 5% from contacting employers directly
- 1% through answering advertisements
- 3% by all other means

So, in today's environment of faded loyalty and greater competition, just how should you approach your next career move? The reality is that job hunting can be handled on a more convenient and predictable basis. However, there are some requirements.

The Princeton/Masters system for finding the right new job

Your starting point is to recognize that the revolution in personal computers, databases, the Internet, and other sources of information can have a dramatic and positive impact on your potential for job-hunting success. So it's essential to capitalize on the remarkable communication and information tools that are available. They truly make it possible for you to take control of your own career destiny.

We believe in a system that emphasizes new and well-organized approaches for going to your markets. We call it "proactive" rather than passive job hunting. To begin with, you need to be willing to put aside your old ideas on job hunting. You need to bring a positive attitude to the table, a will to succeed, and a commitment to taking the necessary action to ensure your success. Here are the steps that are part of our professional job-hunting system.

Marketable assets. The first step involves uncovering all your marketable assets. There is more to this statement than meets the eye, and we will address ways for expanding your marketability beyond your obvious credentials. You will also be introduced to our concept of a personal communications plan—a key element in political campaigns and equally important to making every career search a success.

Career and industry options. The second step involves knowing your options. Many people have found that crucial career or industry changes have brought them more challenge and satisfaction. Chances are, you can uncover new career and industry options, as well as advanced opportunities within your career path.

Superior resumes and letters. This is extremely critical. A series of superior biographies, in combination with some custom marketing letters, can easily bring you 700% to 1,000% more activity than one standard resume and cover letter you might have used. In short, the right written materials can dramatically impact your career possibilities.

An action plan for getting interviews. If you have a plan, you'll know which types of actions to take, and where, when, and how. This material will review the major channels you should consider and the basics of what you should do.

A game plan for interviewing. Let's face it, for every situation, there are likely to be a number of others under consideration. So obviously you must come across better than others. With our system, you'll find a series of steps which will allow you to maximize your chemistry in every interview and to handle objections in the smoothest possible way.

A negotiation process. We will introduce you to an easy-to-use process for negotiating. It has been all that many others have needed.

In summary, methods from the 80s don't work very well anymore. But, then again, old marketing approaches don't work in any field. In recent articles, *Harvard Business Review*'s "Marketing is Everything" and *Business Week*'s "Value Marketing," both emphasized that smart marketing requires doing different things. Sony's founder, Masaru Ibuka, said, "The key to success for Sony, and to everything else in business, is never to follow the others." This is also sound advice for every job seeker.

Never fall victim to these job-hunting myths

<u>**Famous Last Words**</u>

"My friends say I'll do great."

"Sending out a lot of resumes is all I need."

"I can always get a job with my contacts."

"I'm just going to answer ads."

"Recruiters will be after someone like me."

"If I get the interview, I'll get the job."

"My resume is not the problem."

<u>**Famous Last Excuses**</u>

"The economy is so bad. There are no jobs out there."

"My field is slow, and I can't change careers."

"I just don't have the right contacts."

"I can't find any leads."

2
How to Expand Your Marketability

Professional-level job hunting is about gaining a competitive edge. The key is to capture everything about yourself that is marketable, and then build appeal beyond your obvious factual credentials. Here are some thoughts on how to do it.

Are you thinking that your credentials are so strong, your resume so good, that a job will be yours for the asking? Maybe it should be that way, but surprisingly, the "best-qualified" people don't always make the winner's circle. Who does? Those who do the best job of marketing their strengths, their skills—themselves.

If you are like most people, you can increase your chances through a very simple point of view. It has been said time and again by psychologists, motivational speakers, spiritual leaders and coaches, that the most restrictive limits you face are those you put on yourself. So, if you really want to be a serious candidate for a better position or a new career, don't put any limits on your thinking.

We have learned that everyone's experience is more marketable than they realize. In this discussion, we will review a number of ways to broaden your view of your total experience.

Your knowledge, personality, character, interests, and enthusiasm are all marketable

First, assume that all aspects of your knowledge are marketable. For example, do you have knowledge of a job, a product, a process, or a market? It could come from work, hobbies, alumni relationships, reading, or from suppliers, customers, friends, or your social life.

Personality, of course, is just a word for that mysterious combination of traits that can either attract us to someone quite strongly, or on the other hand, leave us unimpressed. More employment decisions are based on personality and chemistry than any other factor. When this happens, the employer is probably thinking: *"He's certainly professional and quick-thinking. I like him, and better yet, I trust him. He'll get along with our team and provide leadership. I need to get him in this firm."*

Your interests and enthusiasm are also marketable. How many employers do you suppose hire people primarily because they showed great interest in their business? *The answer is, a lot!*

The opportunity you represent is also marketable

If you can make an employer aware of an opportunity that you can exploit, or a problem that you can help solve, you can create a job for yourself. Of course, some people view their previous jobs as having a narrow focus, and you may be thinking, *"I don't have a lot of options."* However, you can expand your appeal and uncover more options. The idea is to uncover "any experience you've had" in a way that makes the experience more transferable. Here are some thoughts.

Besides your functional experience, your transferable skills are marketable

Identifying transferable skills is critical. For example, analyzing, organizing, group presentation skills, problem solving, and so on. In the current job market, employers are clearly placing a premium on men and women who are versatile. The parameters around many jobs have changed as layers of management have been eliminated. Those who are perceived as being of great potential value are those who can move from project to project, handling assignments that draw upon different skills.

Because it is unrealistic for people to think in terms of job security, the best way to currently protect yourself and your career is to be seen as a versatile team player capable of being a "money maker" in many different situations. In fact, it is a rare individual who can move ahead and stay ahead with a single predominant skill.

Naturally, your experience can also be reviewed according to various "functions" that apply to most businesses, such as sales, production, accounting, marketing, human resources, etc. At the same time, you need to think of your experience in terms of "action verbs" that describe what you did, and that translate those activities into achievements. For example, *controlled, scheduled, wrote, improved, reshaped, built, created*, etc.

The more ways you describe your experience, the more you will qualify for jobs in many career fields and industries. That's because all organizations are basically involved in similar functions. So, look at your experience from a few different slants.

Having a communications plan is very critical

Political candidates anticipate questions on issues and formulate carefully-thought-out position statements to guide their answers. You need to do the same thing.

Our philosophy involves identifying the "core" words and phrases that will be the heart of your communications plan. These words should become a regular part of "your story" that you communicate to employers, recruiters, and others who might be of help. Please realize that your "tickets" alone (advanced degrees, blue-chip background, titles, etc.) will not necessarily motivate another employer to hire you. Those credentials offer only one form of reassurance that suggests you are right for the job.

Now, when any of us recruit people, we usually have a concept in mind. In the final analysis, we hire others for the skills and abilities that certain key phrases imply. So, it's important to select those that set you apart. For example, you may have *"operated effectively under pressure."* Perhaps you are *"an excellent motivator"* or you may have *"built highly effective teams."* Most people can identify at least 20 key words and concepts. Used appropriately, these words and concepts can set you apart from the competition and convey the unique advantages you have to offer.

Make sure your leadership appeal is evident to others

Much has been written about America's search for leadership at all levels of business. And if there is one quality you want to be able to communicate, leadership ability is it. But just how is leadership projected, especially if you're not a celebrity in the business world?

An article that appeared in United Airlines' in-flight magazine examined the qualities necessary to be perceived as a leader in today's environment. The observations included much of the following: Most experts say that real leaders possess and communicate real convictions. These are seen as strong feelings and principles that have grown with them over time. Obviously, those convictions need to match the requirements of the organization and those who might follow.

Whether it's justified or not, leadership is also attributed to those who create an image of operating at the far edge of the frontier—where new products and solutions are being planned for the future. We tend to think of leaders as those who have vision and the ability to develop new things or bring the best improvements to older ones.

Other attributes that people ascribe to leaders are that they are creative, intuitive, and passionate, and that they project integrity, trust, and boldness. Image, attitude, appearance, and presence can all play a role. Put all of these traits together, and they represent most of the criteria that contribute to people being viewed as charismatic.

The right stories need
to be part of your plan

Most people who interview you will forget what you say in a matter of minutes. To ensure your points are both memorable and credible, use our SODAR technique for creating interesting "stories." This acronym that stands for Situation, Opportunities, Duties, Actions, and Results. It represents a process of describing your past experience. Here's how you can use it:

Situation. Describe a job by reviewing the situation when you began, making it sound interesting. **Opportunities.** Then bring up the challenges the job presented. **Duties.** Subsequently, describe your duties. **Actions.** Importantly, you should quickly move to actions taken by you and others (the team). **Results.** Then relate what results occurred.

SODAR allows you to "tell the whole story." If a SODAR story is well told, it will generate more genuine interest than any recitation of duties. Of course, the R in SODAR (results) is the most important. Try to quantify the results.

Indicate any good things you did to help your organizations and how you took on extra tasks. Describe how you helped your superiors meet their goals, and also the results they achieved. Develop stories that cover situations where you can demonstrate the value of fresh thinking as a means to improving productivity, or show that you have solved a wide variety of problems in diverse areas.

Age doesn't need to be the barrier you think it is

The biggest concern about marketability for many people has to do with their age. As American business has been getting leaner over the last decade, there has been a noticeable trend toward the hiring of younger professionals. A look at the Annual Report issued by PepsiCo, Inc., one of America's top 20 corporations in market value, gives perhaps a good example:

CEO of Pepsi Cola, North America	age 49
CEO of Frito Lay, Inc................	age 46
CEO of PepsiCo Foods/Beverages, Int....	age 44
CEO of Pizza Hut, Inc.	age 51
CEO of Taco Bell Corp..............	age 49
CEO of Kentucky Fried Chicken	age 42
CEO of PepsiCo Restaurants, Int.......	age 42
CEO of PepsiCo Food Systems	age 46
CEO of PepsiCo Worldwide Rest's.	age 50

The same report listed 36 corporate officers of PepsiCo, Inc. The median age was 47. The new CEO of PepsiCo, Roger Enrico, is 51.

Obviously, age will affect job seekers, but this too can be handled. As a general rule, a far more aggressive action plan for getting interviews will be required.

Now from a professional viewpoint, there are different things that we undertake to help our clients get the most out of their marketability. However, they all have to do with the principles of dealing with the factors brought up in this discussion. We start by asking our clients to complete a *Career History and Marketability Profile* (CHAMP).

A remarkable device, it gives us insight into people by having them check words and phrases that might describe them, their achievements, their skills, and their approaches to various situations. Through it, people take a fresh new view of their career experiences. Independently, your approach should be the same.

Lets recap the primary ways for expanding your marketability. First, you can broaden your appeal by communicating your experience according to (a) business functions, (b) your skills and duties, and (c) your achievements. In addition, because your knowledge and interests are marketable, it's essential to surface any special interests that might appeal to employers. Naturally, your personality, character, and enthusiasm can also be marketable (something many people overlook), as well as the opportunity you represent and the types of problems you can help an employer solve.

A major key to building appeal beyond your credentials is the use of a "communications plan." Here, you identify words that reflect your special strengths. Then, you develop the key phrases that describe your traits, skills, abilities, and qualities that employers look for. You follow through by using them in all written and verbal communications. To make your experiences more interesting and memorable, use them with the storytelling concept I've described.

3

How to Uncover the Right Industry Options

More professionals than ever change industries. In fact, in the course of an average career, people will generally work in three or more industries. When you run a professional career search, don't ever short-change yourself by taking a narrow view of your industry options.

For better or worse, in our world of work you will quickly find that when compared to a decade ago, you have changed, your career field has changed, and your industry has changed. In today's market most people must be prepared to market themselves with sufficient skill so that they may be viewed as attractive to employers in a variety of industries.

Why not consider growth industries? What are some of the fast-growing industries? Well, they include such industries as personal computers, software, microchips, entertainment, telecommunications, certain media, biotechnology, physical therapy/fitness, special education, security/private investigation, sports, and anything to do with the Internet, to name a few.

In 1982, the personal computer industry was a $1 billion industry. Today, it is estimated to be more than a $150 billion industry. During this period, the industry has had many ups and downs, but total employment has dramatically expanded.

While many firms have been through profit squeezes and layoffs, an individual who joined an industry during the last decade would now have a substantial range of employer possibilities competing for his or her talents.

Another reason for seeking out growth industries involves their need to go outside their industry to meet their staffing needs. For example, in the early 80s the cable television industry was in a phase of explosive growth. The CEOs of these firms could not find enough people with cable experience to meet their growth objectives. As a result, opportunities abounded for high-level professionals from varied backgrounds. These firms simply hired the best natural talent.

80% of all job seekers consider new industry options

New companies are springing up everywhere, and most organizations are reexamining the way they do business. Medium-sized firms are expanding. New industries now exist that are employing tens of thousands.

Needless to say, the more you appear to know about an industry, the easier it is to generate interviews. For example, do you have experience in or knowledge of similar product lines, distribution channels, manufacturing methods, or problems within an industry? There can be other similarities. Consider the scope of operations, the role of advertising and promotion, the importance of the field-sales organization, or the influence of labor. The harder it is to demonstrate knowledge of an industry, the less likely a person is to move into it. Here are some industry changes that are commonplace:

A client of ours was in marketing with a tobacco company, and she joined a cosmetics firm. Why? Their methods of marketing were similar. Another client was the EVP of a circuit-board company, and was recruited to become president of a firm that makes power packs. Why? These industries have similarities in manufacturing and sales.

If you have no knowledge of an industry but would like to explore situations, extra steps are recommended. The easiest way to acquire knowledge of a new industry is to read trade publications. It's surprisingly easy to be able to communicate on new products and the major challenges as seen by industry leaders.

Another way is to talk with people already in the field. You can go further by getting more formal input, attending trade shows, and the like. The most radical approach is to accept a lower-level job in an industry in order to acquire knowledge.

Now, troubled industries can also have something to offer. During the last decade we've witnessed declines in a succession of industries. However, you should never overlook opportunities in troubled industries. Those who learned lessons in competitive battles can be veterans in any industry.

Transition to a new industry is much easier than it used to be. Historically, people tend to overrate the barriers and to underrate their own abilities to make contributions in new areas in a relatively short time frame. As you review potential industries, you might also remember that while glamorous high-tech and service businesses receive 90% of the publicity today, many people will find far more opportunities in industries that are considered low-tech or non-glamorous by today's standards.

Confidence is critical—
don't underrate yourself

Never overlook your leverage power—the added benefits you may bring by virtue of your contacts or knowledge. You may be able to bring a complete team with you, or perhaps you control accounts who would give you their business in a new field. Or it's possible you have cut millions from overhead before and can do it again.

Your versatility can also be a major consideration. The fact is, nearly every capable person can work in a different function that is broader, narrower, or in some way associated with a past position. Here are some examples that will reinforce this point:

A versatile purchasing manager found it easy to move to a position where she is responsible for all manufacturing; and a advertising manager became the marketing VP for a consumer goods firm in another industry. A general manager switched to big-ticket computer sales because of his experience; and a lending officer became the top executive in a financial services firm.

Be sure to communicate the scope of your knowledge. Sales executives, for instance, usually know quite a bit about marketing, human resources, and distribution. Manufacturing professionals often know a great deal about administration, the control function, and general management. A controller may often have a grasp of every aspect of his/her business.

When you are discussing the requirements for a position, it will be important for you to distinguish between arbitrary requirements and those that really relate directly to results. Arbitrary requirements include degrees, length of time in positions, previous titles, and specific industry experience. However, the final hiring decision usually has little to do with specifications. If you can present yourself convincingly as being able to produce results, you will likely get the job. Here are some more examples:

An executive went from government to president of a pharmaceutical company; and a lawyer from the steel business became EVP of an engineering company. The CEO of a public corporation became president of a Wall Street firm; and the EVP of a utility became COO of a diversified manufacturer.

There are thousands of examples. If you believe you can produce direct results in a given situation, be sure you lay claim to it. Too many people seek out positions at a lower level than they should, or they rule themselves out of a job they could do well simply because they have never done it before.

If you are switching industries, you will find that, generally speaking, more opportunities emerge in the small and mid-sized companies. They don't have layers of management waiting to fill new opportunities. Also, their executives tend to be less specialized, making it possible for you to fill a more versatile role.

To recap, many people are afraid to move out of their industry specialty. However, every month thousands of executives start careers in new industries— areas where they had no direct previous experience. Once you've had experience in two or three industries, your marketability is also greater than before.

Here's some simple advice, but it has worked for people at all ages who needed to make a career change. Get involved in a new career or industry while you are employed. Build your knowledge base by becoming a professional consultant, contract worker, or temp on a part-time basis, or start a small business in your spare time. If necessary, work for a few months as an apprentice and perhaps even without income or on a modest commission. Before long, you'll have developed the knowledge and confidence, and you will be all set when it comes to new options.

For each of our clients, we have a process of analysis for coming up with areas they should explore. It starts with a review of thousands of industries. Then, we use many sophisticated databases to screen the hundreds of smaller or faster-growing industries that might be of interest in each individual case. The end result is that having analyzed someone's background and by applying the type of thinking described in this chapter, we are able to come up with a range of industries for which they might be good candidates.

Most people are unaware of the enormous range of industries that are growing rapidly. When you screen industries as possibilities for yourself, the process is just as I've outlined in this discussion. Essentially, you are looking for some similarities to the areas in which you've had experience. These can take the form of similarities in distribution channels, marketing and sales approaches, manufacturing, whether they are capital intensive or people intensive, and so on.

4

The Only Style of Resume
You Should Ever Use

People who go into the job market with an assembly-line resume will wait a long time for lightning to strike. The higher you go, the more likely you will require several biographies and a variety of custom letters. They need to tell just the right story and be all set for use with the different opportunities that are likely to present themselves.

"Why don't you just pick out the resume that looks the best?"

Your need for a superior resume operates in reverse order to the following criteria.

First are those who have achieved celebrity status. Then there are those who are well-enough known, or who have relationships that help them land jobs immediately. Next are those who have an industry hook or high-demand specialty. Last are the top producers in any field, the people who can simply call and say, "This is what I've done for others, I'm a pro, I can do the same or better for you."

Now if you fit into one of the above categories, you are in good shape. If you are in the other 97%—then the information that follows is very important. The number of resumes circulated, relative to the number of attractive positions, is going up. As I've said, hundreds of people are apt to answer every good ad, and as many as 4,000 resumes arrive at executive search firms each month. In short, the competition is intense and will continue to increase.

When you look for a job, you are reduced to how you look on paper. Nevertheless, 95% of all resumes are average in appearance, disclose too many liabilities, and are rarely interesting. Worst of all, a single resume is usually expected to work with all types of audiences, and it doesn't.

A narrative style of resume is the best of all

After reviewing hundreds of thousands of resumes, we have a good handle on what works best for professionals. The answer: narrative resumes that are written in a style that is similar to a letter.

The first reason a narrative is preferred is that it seems like less of a sales pitch than traditional resumes, which are full of dashes, bullets and too much bold type. I know how much our clients want good jobs, but one of the keys is to never appear too available. Who wants to hire someone who appears desperate or isn't wanted by others? The resumes that work best are ones that make you sound articulate, that never simply scream a bunch of facts, and that tell a persuasive story.

The second reason a narrative is best is that it appears more dignified and more professional. Needless to say, the closer it comes to a letter, the more personal and readable your resume will seem. At the same time, a narrative approach enables you to more easily avoid disclosing any liabilities you may have (things that might rule you out and you'll never know why).

The third reason in support of a narrative is that it is a "solution resume." Using this style, it is easier to craft a story in support of any objective you have. The same holds true for all the letters you might need in a job search. Once you have your narrative, adapting the same words and phrases to marketing letters is much easier as well.

A narrative resume will work best in the four situations that you are likely to encounter. One is when it is requested after you meet an employer—at the beginning of or during an interview. Another is when your resume is used as a leave-behind—after you've finished an interview, and when it is likely to be circulated to other people along with the impressions of the first party. A third is when it is provided for personal contacts to distribute. And a fourth is when it is sent out cold to employers or recruiters.

If you give a moment to thinking about these situations, looking at all the other styles you might use, you'll quickly see why a narrative is really the best solution—and truly the resume for all seasons.

The four popular ways to
arrange your resume presentation

The historical approach. This outlines your career in chronological order, starting with your most recent employer. It works best for those whose careers include a succession of increasingly responsible positions. Clearly it is preferred for the simple reason that it is far easier to read than information presented in other formats. If you want action from recruiters, an arrangement that reveals your factual history in a clear fashion is a must.

The achievement approach. This is most commonly used by people whose main accomplishments may not be in their most recent position. Here, your achievements are listed in the most persuasive language possible, with specific numbers, time-frames, and percentages used when describing them.

The functional approach. This communicates your career experience according to "business functions" (sales, accounting, etc.) It's great for generalists, career changers, people who were with one firm a long time, and those with too many jobs. This same functional style can be used to emphasize skills rather than functions; for example, your experience and achievements in directing turnarounds, boardroom presentations, complex analytical assignments, organizing new companies, etc.

The situation approach. This tells a story about four or five key situations. It gives fast-moving explanations of those situations and how you dealt with them. This format can be very effective for individuals who may be strong generalists as well as those in the highest echelons of corporate America.

Regardless of which of the arrangements you choose, an objective at the top of your resume, along with a short but compelling summary, is critical. This tells the reader that you are a person with a clear purpose, and it enables an employer to quickly assess you in terms of positions that may be available.

In your summary, you may choose to emphasize positive information on any aspect of your story, although most people will want to describe only work experience, education, and their most important personal assets. Having an objective and a summary will help ensure that your main selling points will almost always be read.

Too often people understate their contributions. So, take credit for larger achievements when you have played a key role in the overall effort. It's also important that you be presented as more interesting than your competition. You may also want to comment on issues that have emotional appeal; for example, commitment, values, motivation, professionalism, reputation, work style, and interpersonal skills, among others.

The number of biographies that many executives require today

In today's competitive job market, you cannot run a sophisticated marketing campaign and expect one resume to be effective with each and every audience. To maximize interest in our clients, we typically create the following package of creative materials for each executive.

A CEO / board member biography

Optional. This document is essential only for those executives competing for six figure positions. It tells each person's complete story, often being three or four pages, and is written in a third-person style. It can be very effective when circulated to high-level networking contacts, as well as CEOs, board members, heads of venture capital firms, and other senior people.

More dignified than other resumes, this biography should also be supplied in situations once you are definitely under consideration. Since at that point your material will be carefully read, you want to put your best foot forward. Using a longer story can also help speed things along, and sometimes negate the need for further checking on the employer's part.

A mainstream biography

Required for all professionals, managers and executives, this is the primary or mainstream resume. A highly distinctive narrative resume, it is usually two pages in length. It would be the document used in connection with direct mail, everyday networking, and in various situations where a resume is requested or advisable for introductory purposes.

A recruiter resume

Required for all professionals and executives, this is necessary to achieve satisfactory effectiveness with recruiter mailings. Here a factual and historical approach to highlighting your most marketable assets and skills is required. For senior executives, once a recruiter shows interest, a CEO biography would be supplied.

A spot opportunity resume

Required for all professionals and executives, this document is graphically designed to allow room to conveniently pen a short note on the resume. People use this when they see a news event that suggests their experience could be of help. Handwritten notes allow people to get more of these in circulation, and more quickly. The informal, but personal, handwritten style is very effective.

Universal biographies

Optional. This is a term for resumes we supply to broaden a person's background, and qualify them for other opportunities. For example, a CFO may wish to explore senior operations positions, or a marketing VP might want to be considered for general management jobs. Separate resumes are often required.

The importance of your resumes and letters in a professional career search

It may surprise you but *marketing letters* can often be just as important as resumes. For each of our clients, we typically draft about a dozen custom letters... with each one intended for use with a specific application. For example, we draft separate letters for answering ads, for sending in response to articles, for contacting influential people, for requesting a reference, for using in direct mail, for asking for referrals from acquaintances, for contacting recruiters, and so on.

Having everything prepared in advance is critical, so that our clients can focus on their campaign, rather than attempting to create materials when a situation arises. The goal is to help people respond to situations with more speed and convenience, and most importantly, with greater confidence and bottom-line results. On your own, you should approach your creative materials in the same manner—have them all drafted in advance.

Considering what's at stake with your career, your biographies need to be just right. Your communications must never undersell your capabilities or position you in an overly narrow manner.

The kind of writing that is needed is not something that can be handled with an average effort. Remember, you are marketing a million-dollar product. What's required to do the job at your level starts with taking the time to analyze your career situation and all that you have to offer the marketplace. Obviously, you need to be clear on what your objectives are, and you need to have a way with words to create the documents you need.

There are two guiding concepts to this type of writing. First, it isn't just words that make the difference. The key is in the psychological impact beneath the words—the "subtleties" which help to motivate the right reaction at the receiving end. The second guiding concept concerns the fact that the unpublished job market is a "dormant" market, and remains so until triggered into responding. This happens when you use superior materials to contact the right person, in the right company, and at the right time. Now, unlike standard resumes, narratives can be tailored to create an image about you that says you are interesting, have certain skills and personal qualities—and that you simply are not like everyone else.

Your written materials also assist in other ways, even impacting the interviewing process. Here's an example that illustrates this point. Let's assume a company invited a typical job seeker for an interview. Now, when that person walked in, chances are that they would only be 10% sold, and 90% of the hiring decision would rest on their ability to interview. This could put them under a lot of pressure.

To reduce pressure, your materials should be aimed at pre-selling you to the point of being 40–50% pre-sold into a position, rather than the customary 10%. The idea is to have employers sincerely want to see you. The reaction you want is, "John, I've been looking forward to seeing you. I have the feeling you can really be of help."

In closing, make sure your written materials are the very best they can be. They must be persuasive, visually distinctive and, of most importance, they must capture the best expression of your experience, skills, and potential.

5

The Fastest Way for Finding Good Leads

90% of all jobs are unpublished. However, these unadvertised openings are signaled by events that are reported in the media. Here's the easiest way to find them.

The following discussion is especially important for people who want to change careers or industries. Why are over 90% of all jobs filled privately, and how do companies do this? Well, they seek to fill openings privately because it is an effective and less expensive method for finding quality people.

Most firms fill positions through personal referrals or by hiring someone who simply contacts them at the right time. By hiring in this manner, they avoid the costs of recruiter fees and advertising expenses.

Now, if you can learn where these openings exist, it stands to reason that you can have a major edge over your competitors. What's more, you might be able to have your credentials up for singular consideration, instead of applying right along with scores of others.

To find employers with unadvertised openings, all you need to do is follow events in the press. We call those situations "emerging opportunities." Of course, you can also uncover jobs that are not advertised through mailings, telemarketing, and networking, but following events in the press is the most direct way.

The right events are your key to uncovering emerging opportunities

Every day, in thousands of firms, events occur that ultimately lead employers to begin the process of privately looking for new people. These events are often reported in local and national business publications, trade magazines, newsletters, and newspapers. Here you will find articles on growth situations, new divisions, new facilities, new products, reorganizations, acquisitions, high-level executive changes, and plans for investments or expansion.

For companies undergoing these transitions, chances are they will need to attract good people to handle problems or capitalize on their opportunities. The activity in these companies won't usually be limited to one or two functions either.

While private openings are being filled by all types of employers, they are filled with far greater frequency in organizations experiencing significant change. Here's how a few executives have capitalized by uncovering openings through events:

❏ A financial executive learned that a troubled manufacturer was divesting a division. She called the new president and arranged to meet him. Four weeks later, she became the CFO of this company.

❏ A marketing manager read that a European firm bought a local company. He wrote to express interest and suggested a dialogue when officials visited. Twelve weeks later, he was VP-Marketing, USA, at $120,000.

When you read about a company that is giving off signals that it may be hiring at an above-average rate, don't stop at the obvious implications. Use "ripple-effect thinking." This is simply taking the time to think about all of the changes that may be occurring in the company—up and down the line and across many functions.

You may also get some good ideas about using information that you read about one company to find opportunities with a company's suppliers, customers, and even their competitors.

To take full advantage of emerging opportunities, consider the following example: You read that a manufacturer is starting a division to sell a new kind of packaging for protecting sensitive healthcare supplies. The obvious implications are that this company could very well need people in marketing and sales. Because it's a new division, you might also expect that there will be some need for accounting and finance people as well.

If you're a packaging engineer, you might also project a need for that capability to support the sales effort. Those possibilities would be real enough, but now use "ripple-effect thinking" to see if we can infer some other needs. For example, you may be someone who is experienced in dealing with regulatory authorities. You recognize that the potential sellers of this product will have to deal with them to gain product approval.

When you are seeking out new opportunities, you also don't want to overlook organizations with problems. Problems often imply one of two things: managers haven't been performing well, or the company needs to develop new capabilities in order to survive and grow.

Organizations with problems often need help from the following types of people: marketing people who can identify new markets and launch new products; financial executives who can cut costs or raise capital; general managers who can take responsibility; COOs who can supply new leadership; human resource executives who can help find all these other people.

Most of the time a CEO or a board member will be the logical person for you to contact. Keep in mind that many employers undergoing change are actually the smaller and faster-growing firms, and they are far less constrained by hiring traditions common to major companies. Organizations that are on a fast track will usually be looking for executives with the best natural ability and who have enthusiasm, dedication, and the right work ethic.

How to find events that are good leads to unadvertised jobs

For our clients, we access special databases that report on tens of thousands of business events that are written about in hundreds of media. We retrieve extracts by keywords, such as mergers, executive changes, sales growth, new products, and many other criteria. As reviewed in this chapter, these articles can often be your very best lead sources. Throughout your search, you need to stay abreast of emerging situations as identified in the business section of your local papers and in trade magazines. Remember, information is power, and that's exactly what news of emerging opportunities provides.

How to Make the
Most of Recruiters

The chances of recruiters filling a job that is just right for you, at the moment you contact them, is a little like finding a needle in a haystack. However, recruiters still represent up to 9% of the market. Here's how to make the most of your opportunity with recruiters.

There's no question that recruiters can be of help to your career. But, if you send them an unsolicited resume, the chance of their working on a job that is just right for you at the moment you contact them is very small. However, you can improve your odds by using superior materials and by mailing to larger numbers of the right recruiters.

Executive search firms typically fill positions from $60,000 to $300,000 and up. Many people refer to them as headhunters, and their assignment is to find qualified candidates who meet highly specialized criteria.

For the most part they are retained for searches on an exclusive basis, and they charge their employer clients 30% to 33% of the annual compensation of the position they are seeking to fill. To distinguish themselves in their industry, they are sometimes referred to as "retainer recruiters."

The number of job openings they control is sizable, but still only 9% of the market. Furthermore, on a national scale, a relatively small number of firms control much of the business, even though there are upwards of 7,000 recruiters who claim to be active in the field. Certain recruiters enjoy considerable prestige, often working only on select, high-level assignments. However, there are also many very fine smaller firms who specialize in just a single industry or several industries or disciplines.

On a personal level, recruiters are usually articulate professionals who have a broad knowledge of business. The successful people in the field are generally excellent marketing people themselves.

How do recruiters find candidates? Recruiters have a preference for achievers, people who make strong first impressions and who are successfully employed in other firms. These are the individuals who are most presentable to their clients and who are easiest to sell to them.

Their sources for finding people range from directories and articles in the press to their own broad-range contacts and files of resumes. Of course, the preferred relationships with these firms are the ones that begin with their contacting you. Being visible in your industry is the major key to success with recruiters. Being in a hot field or industry can improve things still further.

If you have kept track of the recruiters who have called you in the past, one of the first things you should now do is renew these relationships.

To get results through a mail campaign, a superior summary of your qualifications is essential. Keep in mind that recruiters are "assignment-oriented." They will be focused on filling their active contracts. In most cases, all that will happen is that you will simply be getting into their files.

At the executive level, mailings of 300 or more are common, and should go out at the beginning of your search. A historical arrangement of your background will normally produce the most response. Keep records of all replies. Using impressive materials, over a six-week period you can expect positive response that will usually range from 1% to 4%—depending on your field, industry, and income level.

If your correspondence fails to supply a phone number that is answered during normal business hours, you will lose many leads. Voice-mail service or an answering machine is a must. Another point to remember is that a second mailing to the same list 10 to 12 weeks later usually produces equal results.

Keep in mind that many large firms are contacted by 50 to 200 job seekers each day. This means there will be instances where recruiters call *months* after the firm first receives your resume.

Regardless, recruiters will be interested primarily in those viewed as marketable, who have blue-chip or high-demand backgrounds, and who have industry knowledge that can quickly help their clients.

You will be most popular with recruiters if you are a person who will explore more attractive situations but who is not too unhappy with his or her employer. Be honest while pursuing a soft sell. If you are desperate or too available, they will never recommend you to their clients.

One last thought on recruiters. In an interview, Duke Foster of *Korn/Ferry*, often considered the largest search firm, indicated that every executive resume they receive is scanned, with one exception. In most cases, if there is no indication of current income or range of desired earnings, your material will never find its way into their national and international database, which is maintained in Los Angeles.

And, by the way, when you visit these firms, you had better be good at interviewing or you may have to write a recruiter off for the balance of your career. Remember, the recruiter is measuring not only how well you are qualified... but how well you will sell.

Uncovering the right recruiters to contact

We provide clients with the recruiters they should contact by screening through databases which cover over 7,000 recruiters. Through these files, we are able to identify various specialists who have the highest probability of being interested in their credentials. Of course, your best prospects will be recruiters with whom you have had a past relationship. Recruiting firms can also be identified in the yellow pages, as well as in published directories.

In summary, recruiters can be very important. However, don't allow more than 10% of your effort to be focused on recruiters. Cover the market with a mailing utilizing superior materials, and consider doing a follow-up mailing 10 weeks later.

7

The Only Way to Answer Ads

Less than 3% of all professional, managerial, and executive jobs are advertised, and the percentage is declining every year. However, there are a few angles that can increase your odds, and there is one key rule you need to follow.

Many of the more attractive advertised openings bring hundreds of responses. This clearly makes answering ads the most competitive area you can tackle.

To make things worse, people use resumes that are average in appearance, disclose far too many liabilities, and fail to highlight why they can fill the advertised position. Rarely interesting or imaginative, they are simply lost among the overwhelming numbers of other candidates. They would do far better by adhering to the number one rule for answering ads—simply send a letter which is tailored to the requirements of the position.

Now, when you start your search, be sure to answer all good ads from the last 13 weeks. A certain percentage of those openings will already be filled, but a number will still be open. This is especially true for higher income jobs. When employers have to screen a lot of applicants, they begin by discarding any resumes that include anything that will rule the person out. That produces a manageable amount of paperwork which is then reviewed more carefully. If you respond five days after the ad appears, rather than when the employer was inundated with paper, your chances of getting a good reading go up rather dramatically.

Here are some additional strategies that can help. We refer to them as downgrading and upgrading strategies. A company advertising for a VP Finance position might be willing to hire a Sr. Accountant who could move up to VP within a year. After all, it isn't so much the title they are after, as the skills and talent. That's an example of downgrading.

By the same token, a company advertising for a Plant Manager might be persuaded to hire a VP of Manufacturing, provided someone could persuade them such a move would be cost efficient and give added capabilities. That's an upgrade.

By the way, did you ever see an ad and feel "that describes me exactly?" Well, as a general rule, if you have not heard anything after two weeks have passed, you should follow up. If you were a good fit for the job, answering ads twice can work.

8

How to Get Interviews
by Direct Mail

Mass mailings don't work. Small custom mailings handled in waves and backed-up by proper telephone follow-up can be very effective. However, never assume it can be done with the wrong targets or the wrong materials.

Some people will tell you that direct mail marketing doesn't work. And, it's true that if you distribute standard cover letters with a resume, or if you use the wrong list, you will be wasting a lot of time and money. However, highly sophisticated and customized mailings can work very well. It takes persuasive writing, the right targets, telephone follow-up, and adherence to proven rules of direct mail.

Every day we are all on the receiving end of direct mail. However bad that mail may look to you, the fact is that the ones you see again and again are working; otherwise, the senders wouldn't be wasting money by repeating the process. Direct mail is a game of testing, revising, and testing some more, until you get the right return for the right dollars. And perhaps the number-one rule in direct mail is that "long copy is the name of the game," because that's what it takes to motivate all of us to action from *unasked-for correspondence*.

The philosophy of direct mail—
"timing is everything"

Let's assume your local lawn mower shop wants you to come in and see a new product it is carrying. Also, let's say that you and your next door neighbor are both out cutting your lawns on a brutally hot day. However, your lawn mower keeps stopping.

Then, the mail carrier arrives at both residences with this long piece of mail that tells you all about a revolutionary new lawn mower, a long explanation of why it's superior to everything else ever manufactured and, guess what, it's available locally. Now, chances are your neighbor will look at the mailing piece for about two seconds and toss it.

Obviously, he isn't in the market for a lawn mower. On the other hand, because the mailing piece has reached you at precisely the right time, it's likely that you will read it quite thoroughly. Perhaps you might be motivated to make a local visit and a purchase!

Now, your position relative to using direct mail is really very similar. Your interest is in reaching the right person who might be in the market for someone like you—right now. No one else counts.

To make direct mail work, you will also need to understand how to use telemarketing in conjunction with direct mail. Of course, few employers will be needing someone like you the day your material arrives. That's why this is a low-percentage response game. The key is to follow traditional direct mail and follow-up rules.

Remember, direct-mail enables you to project your best image, avoid initial disclosure of any liabilities, and make contact that is free from competition. What's more, you have a universe of possibilities to contact.

Putting together your list of high probability targets

You need to decide on a selective list of preferred organizations and people in them to contact. Your "priority list" needs to take into consideration the industries for which you are best suited, your preferred locations, and the size of organization to which you would be most appealing.

In the largest organizations, CEOs or senior vice presidents in charge of specific functions are recommended targets. In smaller firms you will need to reach the top executive or owner.

Your next step is to divide your initial list into three parts according to your "best of best," other "prime choices," and those who are really "secondary choices" you might consider. This carefully tailored target list of employers should be added to as you go through your search. Your goal, of course, is to get an interview with the right person in these organizations, whether you do it by networking, telemarketing, or direct mail.

To make it easy to do this with some speed and convenience, taking advantage of the expanding world of computer databases is a must. Literally dozens of databases are available, any of which can save you time.

Keep in mind that all of them will be at least 10% out of date. Typically, you can select organizations by industry, location, and size and then get information such as the company name and address, telephone number, and names of CEOs and their officers by area of specialty.

Planning your direct mail actions

It's important to do your mailing in waves, over a period of time. You'll get your best response by personally calling everyone you have written. Then, each month you need to assess the results and make revisions to your creative materials as you go forward.

Mass mailings rarely work. People who send out thousands of resumes usually get little to nothing in return. Quite frankly, if job hunting were that simple, everyone would just put their resumes in the mail. Nevertheless, there are mailing firms who advertise, and who will send you copies of resumes that they claim produced fantastic mailing results. Often, these are standard one-page resumes with a one-paragraph cover letter, but the clever marketing approach convinces many that large mass mailings can get them an executive job. *"Caveat Emptor"* or *"let the buyer beware" certainly applies here.*

From our perspective, the key to direct mail success rests with small micro-mailings, using tailored materials for each application, with adjustments made creatively based on the percentage of response (as opposed to the "mass approach," where people often send out standard resumes with a hope and a prayer). Of course, there are certain occupations where you have a limited number of potential employers, for example, musicians, educators, broadcasters, etc. Here, your campaign will be most effective with long-copy letters. Once again, mailings in waves will allow time for selected telephone follow-up.

The types of marketing letters

Keep in mind that when it comes to direct mail, letters can be every bit as important as resumes. You must customize your appeal for each audience. Here are a few pointers that can be helpful.

Cover letters. These should be interesting and brief. Get to the point and make sure they're good.

Letter-resumes. These are stand-alone letters. They must provide sufficient "resume-type information" to stimulate interest. Use them whenever you want to fully tailor the description of your credentials, and avoid revealing any liabilities.

Handwritten memos. These are fast and easy to send off, and executives are used to such notes. If you have some superior resumes that are on-target for your audiences, attaching such notes can work very well.

Letter content. Materials that emphasize what you can do—as well as the results you can bring—are ideal. Next best are letters that talk about your previous accomplishments and the results you achieved. Least effective are letters that list your past experience and work history.

Letter structure. The opening should almost always demonstrate your specific interest (knowledge of the firm, its industry, etc.) and explain your reason for writing. The body must convey your qualifications and potential benefits. Our philosophy is to lead off with each person's best selling-points. Then, we enlarge upon them, presenting our clients as the answer to a need or problem. The closing should restate interest, confirm the desire for an interview, and say when you will be following up.

The mailing approaches
you can choose from

Now, there are many approaches to the mechanics of direct mail itself. For example, let's assume you are seeking a Vice President of Sales position in a large corporation. Here are some of the direct-mail approaches you might consider taking:

❑ High risk. Sent to people by generic titles, e.g. all SVPs of Sales. May result in no response.

❑ Slightly better. Sent randomly to many CEOs. Takes great credentials to work.

❑ Much better. Sent to SVP Sales, selected by industry, size, and location. Good with follow-up.

❑ Very good. Sent to SVP Sales in industries where you have experience; mention it early, and follow up.

❑ Excellent. Sent to SVP Sales to whom you have spoken. Great if you can get your telemarketing on a roll.

❑ Also Excellent. Sent to SVP Sales where mailing goes out under someone else's letterhead.

❑ Outstanding. Sent to SVP Sales to whom you've been referred by someone, with telephone follow-up.

❑ Best. Sent to SVP Sales whom you have met socially or in business, with follow-up.

The essential direct mail rules to follow

❏ Assembly-line materials don't work. Long copy works best, but letters must be crisp. Keep sentences short. Avoid flowery words. Keep paragraphs to five or six lines. Indent the first line.

❏ If you have industry experience, mention it early!

❏ Use the names of both the firm and the individual in the body of your letter. In most cases don't explain why you are looking.

❏ Persuasive letters "read" just like you "speak." Read your letters out loud to see if they need more work.

❏ Personalize your letters by using "I," "my," or "we." Always be enthusiastic. Everyone prefers people who really want to be associated with him/her.

❏ Commit yourself to a telephone follow-up. Name the date and general time you will call.

❏ Never mention your expected income.

❏ Keep records of all direct mail. Follow-up mailings get 80% of the response of your first mailing.

❏ If you have a strong interest in a large firm, consider sending materials to several top executives in that organization.

❏ Use a standard of quality in your materials that is befitting someone at your level.

Direct mail itself is a low percentage response game. The lower your position objectives, the higher the response.

Here is an example of how direct mail was used in two campaigns. It involved two people simultaneously—the EVP and number-two person in a Fortune 200 pharmaceutical firm and the president of a division of the same firm. Both were terminated because of a merger, and both lived in the New York area.

The EVP was moved into a presidency with a division of another pharmaceutical firm in New York inside of twelve weeks. Fewer than 80 three-page custom letters were circulated within the industry—each of which was followed up by phone.

The other person campaigned for 18 weeks before relocating as CEO of a smaller west coast firm. Seven different mailings of 200 each were involved. The key was the seven different letters that were customized to each group.

Finding the right organizations and people to contact

You can't effectively do direct mail without making use of some good databases. We use them to identify the organizations and people who are the highest-probability targets for being interested in our clients. With 10,000,000 employers out there, finding the right targets by metropolitan area, by specific industries of interest, and by growth rates can save weeks of time. As you go through your career search you can also add to your priority list by making the most of a vast number of trade directories.

9

How to Use the Phone

People who are "pros" with the phone are the ones who consistently generate the most activity, and setting interviews over the phone is a lot easier than you think! The phone is your key to getting the right interviews—fast.

Effective use of the phone is easier than you think. However, 90% of all job seekers are reluctant to pick up the phone and make a "cold call." If you're not experienced in using the phone, believe it or not, it's a mostly friendly and he~pful world out there. Most executives are courteous and polite and go out of their way to project a good image of themselves and their company. The same holds true for others such as secretaries or administrative assistants.

Still, there is a certain misconception that all secretaries and assistants will always keep you from speaking with their bosses. They do screen calls, but it is part of their job to make sure that contact is made when appropriate. Throughout this chapter we'll refer to the term telemarketing. The difference between simply making phone calls and "telemarketing" is very basic. When you telemarket, you have specific goals and you use a standardized procedure for making a large number of calls.

Proven telemarketing
guidelines that work

❏ Know how you will be answering your phone. Have answers ready for questions you may be asked. Also, get used to making one call after another. Stand up and you'll give a power assist to your voice. Do your phone work in batches, and you will need only one success to sustain your morale. To warm up, use some throwaway calls to get yourself started.

❏ Prepare a 30-second commercial of your most important selling points. Rehearse it. Tape it and critique it. One of the best times to reach executives is very early in the morning or after 5:00 p.m., when the secretaries have departed. Be prepared for rejection. Effective use of the phone is a numbers game.

❏ Project a natural, confident tone—as you would when talking with a friend. Lower your voice. Speak slowly and never be rushed. Smile while speaking over the phone and your voice will sound more pleasant. Be friendly, enthusiastic and positive. When you encounter objections, stay friendly.

❏ Recognize that the secretary doesn't really know you are or your purpose. If you want advice and information, the decision maker has no reason to shy away from you. When speaking with the secretary, get her name and use it. Be confident and polite.

Approaches for opening
your conversations

The "good news" approach

"Mr. Ellis: When I heard about your four quarters of record growth..." Here you build a positive relationship based on specific "good news." Everyone likes to hear from others who are enthusiastic about their good fortune.

The "third-party" approach

Bill Regan, a partner with Andersen, thought I should get in touch with you. His insights prompted me to follow up with you personally. Do you have a moment?" If you mention the name of a third party who knows the person you're calling, it helps to establish rapport, but it's also helpful even when they don't know each other."

The "specific reason" approach

Anyone who has experience in getting things done can consider using this "specific reason" approach. It's straightforward and can go like this: *"Mr. Franklin, I have a 'specific reason' for calling you. I know the line of business you are in and something of the processes you use. During the past 15 months, I have been able to save a company like yours approximately $850,000. I would like to share the details with you."*

The "Perhaps you can help me" approach

"Hi, Mr. Ellis, I'm Tom Cole. Perhaps you can help me. Since the position has already been filled..." If the individual you contact does not have a precise fit in their department, perhaps they could help you meet a person in another division. If the person you want to speak to is out, the best response is, *"Thanks. Perhaps you can help me. When is a good time to call back?"*

Tips for handling people
who screen your call

❑ Start by using the name of the person who is the "screener." Once a person knows he or she has been identified, their manner will become more personal. When asked your name, identify yourself with an organization if possible.

❑ If you don't get through on your first attempt, and you can't get a suitable time to call back, suggest a time when you will call the screener back. In all cases, until you have established direct contact, don't leave messages.

❑ When you call back, use the screener's name with the receptionist. After establishing that the person is difficult to reach, try this procedure: *"Since he (or she) is so hard to reach, would you do me a small favor? May I call back at _____ to see if he would be interested in speaking with me for a few minutes?"* If you must leave a message, leave one of potential benefit to the person you are calling.

❑ Consider reversing your attempt to speak with the decision-maker by asking for an internal referral to another line manager in the area in which you might want to work for the company.

❑ If the screener refers you to personnel, get the name of the person to whom you will be speaking. Call back later for that person or request an immediate transfer.

❑ After a few minutes of discussion, ask two or three penetrating questions about the company's needs. When asked difficult questions, those who don't know the answer are more inclined to refer you to an appropriate line manager.

❑ After a few days, call back the screener and explain that while the personnel people were helpful, they were not really able to answer the questions you had in mind.

❑ If you encounter the question: "Are you looking for a job?" The answer: *"Yes, I am; do you think you could help me? Though I'm employed, a friend suggested your firm to me."*

❑ Or, if you encounter the comment, "We don't have any openings at the present time," respond: *"I appreciate a person who is direct; however, I have such a strong interest in the firm, I really believe that with your recent growth, I could be a great asset. Will you allow me to tell you why?"*

"We'd like to honor you for being the only job hunter to get through every barrler... and reach our boss!"

After reaching the right person, consider these openers

❏ From your annual report, I read that the company's expanding in the _____field. That's an area where I could help, and I would like to schedule an appointment.

❏ My friend, _____, suggested that I make a point of contacting you. You may recall from my letter that I have experience in _____ that might be of help to you.

❏ With my background in _____ and the recent news about _____, I thought I should try to get in touch with you. Could you suggest a convenient time? Do you have 20 minutes before you get started some morning next week?

❏ Mr. _____, your company has a tremendous reputation for market-leading products. I'd like very much to visit with you to explain how I could contribute to that reputation through my work in _____. Do you have a half hour free this Tuesday?

How to come up with the people to contact by phone

By sorting through our electronic files, we are able to provide our clients with organizations and people they should consider contacting by phone. This is done in the same way we develop recommended contacts for direct mail. You can supplement your contact list through local directories, phone books, and other guides which cover your preferred metropolitan areas and industries. In summary, make it a point to become a "pro" on the phone. Your confidence will soar, and you'll save an enormous amount of time.

10
Networking—The Right Way

There is nothing like personal contacts; however, the people who depend on them too much may be in for a long search. Here are some thoughts on making the most of your old contacts and even building new ones from a zero base.

There's no substitute for personal contacts who can really be of help. The best way to use them is to never ask directly for a situation in their organization.

Of course, most people never get the most out of contacts they may have worked a lifetime to develop. Have you ever heard a person say, *"I've asked all of my friends to be on the lookout"*? They honestly believe they've done everything they can to get help. If they thought about it, they would realize that they've probably approached these friends on a very general basis and asked a favor which is next to impossible. They say, *"Let me know if you hear of anything, Joe."* Joe, of course, will keep his friend in mind, but probably only for a very short time. Five minutes later, Joe is back to his routine, and his friend is forgotten. However, the fact remains that Joe was probably willing and might have been able to help. How do you avoid the same mistake? One answer is to make your request sound important, but to also make sure your communication is a pleasant experience for them.

Remember, people are far more likely to respond if you make it easy for them to assist you. For example, you might ask a past associate if he knows of any top executives among some growth companies you have identified. Or you could ask a financial executive to review recent financial job openings with you and request permission to use his/her name in a cover letter.

On the other hand, you could ask a top person at a former customer to arrange letters of introduction to companies in his field. Then offer to draft a letter. Or, if you know someone in human resources, you could see if he would help by lending his name for contacting recruiters. Let him know the jobs that interest you, the firms that have appeal, and just what you want him to do. The best way to use these people as a source of referrals is to ask their permission to possibly use them as a reference.

An example of a
perfect endorsement

Consider the story of Phil. His boss kept telling him he was worth more, but the firm was losing money. When Phil heard that the company was to be sold, he felt his $60,000 salary was $20,000 less than it should be.

We helped make him aware of the power of his contacts. Would his boss, a good friend, be a good reference? And did the boss feel bad about paying him less than he was worth? Absolutely! Could Phil ask him to be a reference, and would he raise him to a level of $80,000 for his staying the last two months? That's what Phil asked for and got! Now, the boss had a friend who was a partner in an CPA firm. Phil asked his boss if he would approach his friend as a reference. Together, they visited over lunch. Guess what? He was happy to act as a second reference. In the same way, Phil developed a third reference, his brother-in-law.

When he launched a campaign, he had a good interview with the president of a company. The president asked for three people who could speak about him. Phil immediately recontacted everyone, so they were ready. After his boss had given him a glowing reference, the president mentioned that he was still uncertain. When the second person (the boss's friend) was called, he said that in the right situation Phil could help save a million dollars in taxes and cost reductions. He also repositioned Phil, in the eyes of this president, to a broader-based financial executive.

Next, Phil's third supporter endorsed what the others said and added a few points. Within days, he got a call from the president, and guess what? His message was, *"Phil, what will it take to get you?"* Phil ended up with a position as VP finance at $90,000.

How to set up
your references

Most of the time, important references will be the people you reported to, the person you currently report to or their superiors, and, on rare occasions, the people who worked for you. Choose the highest level reference, as long as you get an enthusiastic endorsement, and avoid people who don't communicate well. Even though you may never have worked for them, all types of respected people might be of help.

In most cases, three references will suffice. Be sure to prepare your references with care. Let them know that you have a high regard for their opinions; this will reinforce the positive chemistry between the two of you and make them want to do their best for you. Don't forget that even good personal contacts will know only part of your background. Make sure that they learn the full story.

In most situations, you will provide the names of references rather than letters of recommendation. In the nonprofit and academic areas, however, it is traditional to collect written recommendations.

Another point is that some of your contacts are likely to be your best sources of referrals. When you've really polished your materials, leave them some resumes, and be sure to reassure them that you will not abuse the use of their names. After calling your contacts, send a brief note that shows your appreciation and summarize a few positive things they can say about you. You can even prepare a list of questions that employers might ask and suggest some answers for them.

By the way, be sure to let your contacts know as soon as you have used their name, and ask them to let you know when they have been contacted. This is important because employers will sometimes ask them for someone else who is familiar with you.

In addition to confirming dates and incomes. Assume that employers will want to check with your past superiors. Track these people down for at least the last three jobs or ten years. Don't be reluctant, even if you have not bothered to keep in touch. People like to learn what is happening to others.

In the case of people who have moved into top management, references from any but the last one or two positions are rarely needed. Let the employer know that you need to keep your activity confidential. This lets them know you have a worthwhile position to protect. If you have worked in one company for a long time, contact former employees or bosses who have left your company and ask them to be references. If appropriate, consider using customers, suppliers, or trade group contacts.

Job seekers often struggle with concerns about certain references. It's long been said that a bad reference won't hurt as much as a good one that turns out to be poor. If someone is apt to give you a less-than-glowing recommendation, bring it out in the interview and then supply enough people to offset it. For example, if the interviewer asks to speak with someone who will be questionable, defuse the situation by explaining that you had differences of opinion on some managerial styles. Remain totally objective and unemotional, and never imply negatives about that person.

Also, you might have a friend do a mock reference check to find out what is being said. If the person is neutral, don't hesitate to ask the person to furnish more positive information. As a last resort, you may have to imply that you will seek a legal remedy.

How to network
strangers and influential people

Numerous articles have said that many people have been networked to death. However, the amazing thing is that it still works very well. You need finesse, you need to be very clear about your objectives, and you need to use your time extremely well. By networking effectively, your phone presence, personality, and follow-through can substitute for precisely the right experience. Networking works because every organization experiences turnover—and a great deal more of it than they like to admit. In addition, recruiting is very expensive.

Networking within an industry where you have experience or interests and networking efforts directed to influential people are where you want to concentrate. Governors, congressional representatives, state senators, and other politicians can be excellent sources for referrals. The same is true for prominent doctors and lawyers who speak with many people during the course of each day. Clergy, CPAs, hospital trustees, directors of chambers of commerce or other civic groups, members of industrial development boards, investment bankers, insurance brokers, and many others also fall into this category.

Another option is to expand your networking through business activities. Here you have to increase your visibility. You can expand your business network by visiting places patronized by those in your field, or attending seminars, parties, and supplier meetings.

Trade shows have long been an efficient way to develop contacts. In one location, you usually have dozens of people assembled, and all of them are there because they want to talk to people. Still others have had success by networking through associations. Many professional organizations, alumni, and trade associations act as intermediaries between job hunters and employers. The executive directors of associations, chambers of commerce, and fraternal organizations or Jaycees usually have many "lines" into their communities. They know where growth is occurring.

Professional groups also fund and manage business magazines, journals, newsletters, membership lists, industry directories, and trade show catalogs. The editors at these journals can be influential contacts.

Some everyday networking guidelines

Once you've made contact, one key to successful networking lies in asking the right questions. When probing for information from someone you don't know well, keep the questions broad, and related to the industry. Naturally, you want to know about trends in any business in which you might want to work. They can facilitate the kind of shoptalk shared at a trade conference. Here are some sample questions you might consider asking for general information:

What are the long-term trends in your industry? With those trends in mind, what skills are companies likely to be looking for in new executives? What are some good sources of additional information, either articles and reports, or people to talk to? Who are the active recruiters in the industry? What are the fastest growing areas of the business? When your contact is interested enough to concentrate on your career needs, obviously different questions are appropriate. There are many common errors that people make while networking. Here are some points to remember.

❑ Networking is part of the "job" of looking for a job. List people you want to see, and find a way to get through. Getting through isn't the victory; that comes only after you've completed a successful interview.

❑ Be prepared. Know what strengths to get across.

❑ Talk with people wherever you go. Let people know that you are thinking about a new opportunity. Most people understand when they're "being networked" so you should never try to fool them.

❑ Keep your interviews brief. Ask for ten-minute appointments. Leave every meeting with several new names and make note of the names of secretaries. Send a thank you note after your interview.

❑ Exchange business cards with everyone you meet.

In summary, there's nothing like personal contacts; however, before you approach them, make sure that your goals are clear and your materials are just right. Ask them to be a reference, and, of course, for referrals, and make it as easy as possible for them to help.

11

How to Get an Employer to Create a Job

Firms are creating jobs to fit high-level talent they uncover.

Knowing how to get a job created should be one of your capabilities. Let's face it, everybody is looking for talent if they have benefits to bring them. With a little initiative, many people have created their own destinies.

The "create a job" approach is for people who want a job tailored to their best abilities, or who can readily present themselves as a solution to a problem. A few examples might include a person who can develop new products for a company, a sales executive with contacts in particular markets, or a general manager who can start up a division in a specific industry.

The "create a job" approach should also be considered by anyone who may have difficulty winning offers through other means. This includes those with a narrow market; people who wish to change industries; or those who have been unemployed for a while or who want to stay in a specific geographic or industry area.

Keep in mind this simple thought. Employers hire people whenever they are persuaded that the benefit of having them on board outweighs the dollar cost. The following pages will give you some guiding principles as you consider this approach.

Creating a job—Principle #1
Target small firms and reach people in authority

The first principle to understand is that to have your best chance at creating a job, your highest-probability targets are likely to be small to medium-sized companies. This includes firms that are growing rapidly, bringing out new products, forming new divisions, acquiring other companies, or reorganizing.

These are the firms that need good people, often from other industries. They are free to move quickly. Large corporations are the least likely to respond to this approach. Budgets are allocated, and hiring practices more structured. Of course, there are exceptions. All you need to do is assess your talents and contact the firms most likely to need you. And if you know a market well or have talents in a particular function, just consider the industries where they would apply.

Now you must reach people in authority in each firm you contact. For example, you must be able to communicate directly with the person you would most likely work for, or that person's boss. In small and medium-sized companies, this is normally someone at or near the top. Entrepreneurs, of course, are ideal for contacting in this regard.

Creating a job—Principle #2
Use a benefit proposition

Your benefit proposition must be an accurate, concise, and easily understood description of what you can do. Your message has to hold the promise of tangible value on a scale large enough to warrant an investment in you. In that initial communication, you will also need to establish your credentials. Mention specific results you achieved in the past. They are the best indicators of what you can do in the future. By the way, achievements don't have to be large, but they do have to be significant.

One key point to remember is that if you have an exciting idea to communicate, it may help if you can show how someone else has already used that idea successfully. Dealing with opportunities is a key job for many executives. Most don't have enough time in the day and are predisposed to positive news from people who can help them. They will want to believe your message, so all you need do is make sure you provide positive reinforcement.

By the way, you can get your message across by phone or with a letter. Either way, make sure your "benefit position" is clear, easy to measure, and significant; and be prepared to establish your credentials quickly.

Creating a job—Principle # 3
Identify their problems, needs, and vision

Your initial communication held out the promise of a major benefit. So, when you get the interview, you need to be ready. What are your ideas? What makes you confident they'll work? Do you understand the company's problems? Address these areas, but always convey humility. For example, you might say:

"I hope you didn't find my letter too presumptuous. No doubt you've already given a lot of consideration to these areas." Or... "I'm sure you've talked to many people who thought they knew your business better than you do. I don't mean to come across that way. I have a number of ideas, but let me first pay you the courtesy of listening to your opinion on these areas."

Comments like these set the stage for a cordial exchange. They can allow you to do the three things you need to accomplish in your first meeting: learn what the employer really wants; build rapport; and focus the employer's attention on areas where you can help.

Your first goal is to find out how the employer views the problem. What are the key challenges? What is the "hot button?" Where are the priorities? What attempts have been made in the past?

Make sure you maintain a balanced conversation. Ask questions and make positive comments in response to the interviewer's remarks. Most important, try to get the employer to share his innermost thoughts and vision for the organization. Only when he starts to think about this and the significant achievements he might realize, would he consider the possibility of creating a job. Show your enthusiasm and get agreement for a second interview.

Creating a job—Principle # 4
Stir the employer's imagination

In your second interview you must reinforce your value by drawing a clear picture of the benefits you can bring. Then you need to build enough enthusiasm to get an offer or be asked to speak with others. The employer should begin to anticipate specific benefits and relate them directly to your talents. The focus of the conversation should be on the future, with the employer picturing a company benefitting from your contributions.

A dry recitation of proposed improvements won't be enough. You will have to convey enthusiasm and create a sense of excitement. To do this you will have to refine your thinking, clearly identifying those areas the employer sees as most important. For each of them, be ready to discuss general approaches you would take to reinforce the notion that you will succeed.

Your best way to do this is to tell stories about your past achievements. If you build sufficient enthusiasm, the employer may conclude the meeting with a statement that he'd like to create a job for you. Or, he may ask you to meet with others in the company. If that happens, take the opportunity to build additional enthusiasm with every member of the team.

Creating a job—Principle #5
Consider the report option

If you're not getting interest, you might make an offer to study the situation in more detail, perhaps to observe the company's operations or talk to knowledgeable outsiders, and to come back with a written report. The purpose? To make the entire subject more significant in their mind.

The report should discuss the areas where you would make contributions. For each area, you would want to point out how you would proceed, demonstrating carefully the near-term benefits for the company. If you get interesting input from outsiders or cite examples that support your points, it will make your presentation more compelling.

If you try the report option, stage it properly. Let the employer think it's important and ask for adequate time to present your findings. Your report, of course, would include a recommendation that a job be created.

In summary, top management in most companies are well aware of the expenses involved in recruiting. When someone exceptional comes to their attention, many can act rapidly to create a job situation. They develop a new position or shift someone of lesser talent to make room. Every day, people win positions created this way. You can too.

12

A Plan for Getting Interviews

Job hunting is a numbers game, and a lot of contacts are needed to generate the right number of interviews. However, most people proceed by trial and error. Having a strategic plan will save you a lot of time and money.

We believe in developing action plans for getting our clients interviews. Following an action plan enables them to job hunt with far less strain, confusion, or worry, and keeps them on track. Without one, most people take haphazard actions, hoping that they'll get the results they want.

Today, following a plan makes a lot of sense for anyone who is serious about job hunting. It will help you approach job-hunting actions systematically and will produce far better results. The concept is simple. There are no gimmicks involved. Rather, it is a process for deciding on the number of interviews people want to generate, then backing into a series of job hunting actions that will yield that number of interviews.

Let's review the key elements
in any marketing effort

Consider for a moment how products are successfully sold. In most cases, a marketing plan is followed. The starting point is to *understand* all of the vital product information. As already discussed, people have to dig deep to understand what they have to offer the market.

Next, each product must be *positioned* correctly. This means going after the right career and industry. You seldom see a product that claims it can do everything for anyone.

Then, you must have the marketing tools to *promote* your product. For executives, this means the resumes and letters, the promotional materials you are likely to require. Like advertising, they should all be developed in advance.

Of course, products need be *priced* right so they will sell. While your income potential will ultimately be determined by supply and demand, your negotiation strategy should be determined at the outset.

When a product is ready to go, it needs to reach the market with the right *distribution*. How will you get your message out, and where will it go? How will you come up with the right leads, contacts, and openings? What are the channels for putting your credentials into the marketplace?

Your action plan for getting interviews

As you approach your plan, you will need to first decide on the priority you will give your campaign. If you are out of work, you need to design an aggressive campaign—one that might potentially produce more activity than you really need. Any plan requires a timetable. For most executives, we recommend a 13-week schedule. If it ends up taking longer, that's okay, but start by thinking that you want to reach your goal within this period.

Again, job hunting is a numbers game. The more good contacts you make, the more good opportunities that will come your way. We establish action plans by deciding on the number of situations a client would like to explore. For example, someone might wish to explore at least a dozen situations which, if achieved, might reasonably yield a couple of offers over a 13-week period.

To develop that activity, this hypothetical executive might require a plan with a goal of getting two interviews from six of the following seven channels: (1) from answering ads; (2) from contacting recruiters; (3) through pyramiding personal contacts; (4) through networking influential people; (5) through emerging situations identified in the press; (6) through telemarketing to employers on a direct basis; and (7) from micro-mailings to potential employers of interest.

As you implement your plan, you will need to regularly take stock of your progress. For example, are you keeping up with the plan? Are you getting positive feedback on your materials? Are your goals realistic? Is it time for some fine-tuning or adjustments?

If you don't see yourself zeroing in on the right offer, reevaluate your materials or modify your plan. As long as your goal remains unchanged and you remain committed to reaching it, determination and effort are the keys that will ultimately get you there.

To recap, our philosophy includes developing a customized action plan for every client that we assist. A complete track for running their search, it saves our clients time and money, and can dramatically speed their campaign. So follow a plan that is carefully strategized and that addresses what you should do, week by week. Do it right, and the net result will be that you'll get the right new job in less than half the time.

13

Your Most Important Interviewing Strategy

Job hunting success depends 70% on marketing and personal chemistry and 30% on background and ability. With more people to choose from, employers are increasingly more selective. Your number one interviewing strategy is to build personal chemistry every step of the way.

Getting the right interviews is only half the battle. Let's now discuss just how you can convert interviews into offers at a higher rate than average. Your starting point is to have an interviewing game plan—one in which you conscientiously work at building personal chemistry at all times.

Last year there were far more than 100 million interviews. Think about it! What's more, no two were the same. So how do you prepare? Our philosophy is that you do it the same way you would prepare for a sports contest; there are millions of them and none are the same.

In either an interview or a sports contest, you can't plan precisely how things will go, but you can have a game plan. That means knowing the points you want to touch on and the questions you want to raise. But it's not only what you say that is important. Interviewing involves the exchange of information and the building of personal chemistry.

Building chemistry—Rule #1
Research the firm & get the staff on your side

This leads us to your first step for building chemistry, and it involves researching the company in advance. Did you ever meet a person for the first time who knew a lot about you? It takes you by surprise, doesn't it? It's a great way to make a positive first impression.

Many people have built successful businesses that way. A friend of mine attributes his success to the research he does ahead of time. Four out of every five of his clients tell him that he wins their business because he knows a lot more about them than anyone else.

When you confirm an appointment, use the opportunity to gather more information. Many people have been able to get job descriptions, organization charts, and brochures ahead of time simply by requesting them over the phone. That will help prepare you to be able to build better chemistry in your interview.

Building chemistry with the front-office staff can also make a difference. Can you guess what percent of executives say their secretaries influence them? What do you think? One-third? Half? Well, about two-thirds of them do.

Here's how this might affect you. Not too long ago, I was interrupted by Hattie, who stated that Mr. Baxter had arrived for his two o'clock interview. I had forgotten about the appointment. I immediately asked, "What do you think of him, Hattie?" She didn't say a word. She just gave a thumbs-down signal. That was the end for poor Baxter. So be attentive to those who work up front, and have a conversation that gives you information that will help. You may find that when you go out of your way to be respectful to them, they will often go out of their way to help you.

Building chemistry—Rule #2
Project the right attitude

Building chemistry is also about attitude and image. Psychologists tell us that the way we expect to be treated affects the way we are treated. So build positive expectations about every interview. Of course, when we are on the hiring end, as employers, many of us reach a negative decision in the first five minutes of an interview. Why? Well, if you have the credentials, you've either established a good initial impression or you haven't.

And what determines this personal chemistry? People silently react to the image you project, your posture and body language, the things you say on any subject at all, and the way you answer questions. So consider the kind of image you project. After all, each of us is continually projecting some kind of image. It isn't just physical image or dress, although your appearance speaks before you say a word. It's also a matter of attitude, interest, enthusiasm, and whether you come across as a person as honest, loyal, and in good health.

We tell our clients to check their image before they ever get to the interview, but they shouldn't be too kind to themselves. You might go to someone who is not really close to you and ask them what kind of an attitude they think you project. Ask for their honest opinion of your appearance, eye contact, and mannerisms. Listen to what they have to say; then check out the same things with someone on your side. Somewhere between the two, there will be an accurate picture, and if anything needs to be worked on, do it.

Building chemistry—Rule #3
Compliment others without overdoing it

Do you like receiving compliments? Do you think other people do? You bet they do! So before the interview, read or talk to people about the company and uncover some good things to say. Somewhere in those first few minutes, find the opportunity to let the interviewer know that you heard good things.

This will show that you know something about the company, and it's also what we call a "third-party compliment," where you are passing on the good news that you heard from others. You can compliment their facilities, people, products, advertising, public relations, or many other things.

However, whatever you do, be specific. Don't just say that people you know are impressed by the product. Talk about "why" they are impressed. Maybe it's that new product they added, or the reliability of their products. All of us like to hear about how our products have pleased customers. By giving details, you show that you have given the subject some thought and that your compliment is not just empty flattery.

Building chemistry—Rule #4
Establish rapport as you answer questions

The way you answer questions has more to do with building positive chemistry than with what you say. For example, suppose you get the old standby, the number one question in the world of interviewing: "Tell me about yourself." Many interviews include a form of that question.

You'll want to answer, but chances are you're not sure what they want to hear. You could start out by talking about the kind of person you are and some of your attributes, but that may not be what the interviewer is interested in. Faced with such a dilemma, a safe way out is to self-qualify your answer:

"Certainly, Charles, I'd be happy to tell you about myself, and I'm sure you are interested in my work experience. I'll focus on the past few years and how they relate to this position. I can start with my most recent experience and work backwards if you like."

When you self-qualify like that, you give the interviewer plenty of opportunity to respond, and to direct the conversation toward some other area, if that's not what he or she is really interested in. That way, you can avoid talking for ten minutes about the wrong things.

You will also want to answer questions with good, action-oriented stories. If you fail to tell a story, do you think the interviewer will remember the conversation? Don't count on it. People don't remember answers to questions or concepts. What people remember and what impresses most of them are stories—good stories—action-oriented stories.

When you answer questions, remember to gear your comments to potential contributions relative to sales, profits, cost reduction, efficiency, innovations, quality improvement, etc. When there is a silence, have questions about the field for which you have answers. Create an opportunity to demonstrate knowledge. Being prepared builds confidence and allows you to be more spontaneous. Always maintain eye contact and establish your sincerity and integrity.

When you encounter difficult questions, one way to handle them is with the "U-turn" technique. For example, let's say an interviewer says: "You look very impressive on paper, Carol. If you're this good, you ought to be able to solve all of our problems. Tell me, why should we hire you?"

Now, of course, you know the person doesn't believe you're that good. However, if you begin to talk about why they should hire you, you run the real risk of going on at length about all the wrong things. With the "U-turn" technique, you don't give an answer. Instead, you turn the question around in a way that acknowledges the status of the interviewer and maybe even pays an indirect compliment. Your comment might go something like this:

"I have a lot of experience I believe this firm could use. But it would be presumptuous of me to tell you what you need before I've even shown the courtesy of listening to what you think the priorities are. If you'd be kind enough to share some of your thoughts on these priorities, perhaps I could give a more intelligent answer."

Building chemistry—Rule #5
Keep rapport as you find out what they want

The next area you need to look at has to do with the question of how you find what the interviewer really wants. Sometimes they get directly to the point and tell you exactly what they are looking for. That makes it easy. Put your listening ability to work. One of the easiest ways to impress people is to ask intelligent and penetrating questions about the firm and the position.

Find out what happened to the last person in the job. Ask the interviewer about his experiences and that of his superiors. If a situation stalls, raise questions by simply asking, *what? when? where? why?* and *how?* Find out to whom the position reports and how long that person has been in the job. Pinpoint the authority that goes with the job, and find out what they expect you to accomplish in the first six months.

You could ask a simple question such as, "What would be the biggest challenge I would face?" If the interviewer has some reservations, ask a question that is likely to bring them out. Don't forget—you're better off knowing their concerns so you can deal with them.

Most importantly, find out how the interviewer sees the problem, what the expectations are, and any progress so far. When you do this, you're learning what the unwritten requirements of the job are.

Let's assume that you've asked the right kinds of questions and done enough listening. Now you know what they want. It's time to let them know you have what they want, and you need to build chemistry as you do it. To create this rapport calls for advance preparation, and having your own two-minute interviewing commercial ready to go. Again, the purpose is to let them know you have what they want!

Now it's time to determine if you want the job, and you need to keep building chemistry while you do it. One way to do this is to verbalize a positive summary of the meeting, pointing out your enthusiasm about the job. After the summary, ask a question that will generate feedback:

"In your opinion, are my skills and strengths as closely matched to your needs as I think they are? How can we pursue our interests further?"

If you can build chemistry, as well as let the interviewer know what you want, your success may come down to projecting the right image. You want to be looking good and feeling confident, so be sure to dress well and try to get in the best shape you can. When you have a game plan for building chemistry, you will project confidence from knowing what and how to communicate and being ready to do it.

When we manage a campaign, we feel that having a game plan for interviewing is very important. For each client, we advise them on what to say, or omit, in interviews. We also suggest answers for the difficult questions they may be asked, and recommend questions to raise which help control the pace of each interview. Quite often, we do short video interview training sessions to help get them better prepared. Of most importance, we make sure that each person gets used to concentrating on building chemistry at all times.

In summary, employers need to feel that you are a quality person, and hopefully, exactly what they are looking for. However, thousands of job campaigns have produced convincing evidence that jobs at all levels are ultimately won by those who simply establish the best personal chemistry.

Image building for men...
looking good and feeling confident

This summary is only intended as a brief guideline. However, if you have time, there are numerous books on the subject of dress which are worthwhile reading.

Overall impressions are established within the first few minutes of a meeting. So, before you launch your campaign, assess your wardrobe. You should have a few appropriate "classic" outfits because you must expect to go through a series of interviews. Avoid wearing the same attire twice.

For interviewing, most people will do best if their suits are properly fitted and conservative. A balanced job search wardrobe will ideally include a navy blue suit, a darker gray and a charcoal pinstripe. High fashion styles are not suitable unless you are in one of the "glamour" industries.

One of the most difficult things for most men to do is throw away suits. If your suits are old, give them to charity and take the tax deduction. Wallet, credit cards and other paraphernalia should be kept in a briefcase. This latter practice is more common among top executives. By the way, allow 5" from the tip of your thumb to the end of your sleeve—5 1/4" if you wear cuff links. Don't let tailors persuade you to take longer sleeves!

Clothing must fit properly. This is particularly true with suits, which sometimes slowly shrink with dry cleaning. Be prepared to go back a number of times for alterations, and make sure your pants cuff barely touches your shoe.

As for your shirts, solid colors are recommended, with white and blue being traditional and safe preferences. Wear these colors in the interviews, or until you have the opportunity to assess the working environment you are exploring.

The fit of your shirt deserves special mention. If you have gained weight, you may be wearing your collar too tight. Ex-athletes who have trimmed down will often find that their collars have become loose. A well-fitting collar makes a tie a pleasure to wear for the entire business day. The fit of your cuffs is also important.

The most popular shirt over the years has been the 100% cotton long-sleeved, pointed-collar business shirt. Generally speaking, you will want to avoid short-sleeved shirts unless you live in a warm climate. A word of caution: Be sure that the front and collar are not rippled. This will give you a "sloppy" image. Those who wear cuff links should make sure they are simple. A gaudy look is likely to be perceived as a negative.

Why not buy a few ties? Ties can be fun and can give you a unique look. To a great extent, this element of your wardrobe is a matter of preference. For most people silk ties are best.

The brighter, more contemporary geometric and floral designs also come in a wide array of vivid color combinations that are in good taste. Above all, be sure your tie is clean and fresh in appearance. Bow ties will do little to enhance your image of assurance.

Your shoes should be well polished. Slip-ons are increasingly acceptable but eyelet shoes are still preferred. The old military "spit-shine" can be a real power builder.

Don't underrate accessories. Belts and buckles should be conservative. Socks should be over the calf in length. It is not necessary to have a handkerchief tucked in your breast pocket, but it can be a nice touch. The handkerchief you carry should be clean and pressed. A wallet and briefcase show a lot about a man. *Bulging wallets and oversize briefcases can detract.*

Your hair style should be natural and casual. As a rule, if you appear older than you would like, your hair should be on the short side. *(Short hair will normally give you a younger appearance.)* For most men in their 20s or 30s, however, a somewhat longer look is appropriate.

Be sure your glasses are clean and in good condition. For late afternoon interviews, carry an electric razor in your briefcase and shave an hour or two before. Be sure to have your barber trim facial hairs (including nose and ears) before your meeting. As far as after-shave or cologne is concerned, keep it subtle or don't use it.

For those of you who are overweight, clothes can cover up just so much. Lose some extra pounds if at all possible. If not, stand up straight, sit tall and be yourself. Carry yourself in a way that creates a look of confidence and authority. Remember, when you are job hunting, the people you meet socially can be instrumental in helping you land an attractive new position.

Image building for women...
looking good and feeling confident

Elegant and self-assured—what woman wouldn't want to convey these qualities to an employer? However, to make the best possible impression, make some preparation.

A woman who "looks right" for the job makes it easier for any potential employer to make a positive decision. By creating the best possible appearance, you also enhance your self-confidence. You want to feel great about yourself.

Clothes tell the employer how you see yourself. Your hairstyle and choice of makeup will either reinforce or detract from your professional image. The accessories you choose—shoes, purse, jewelry, etc.—make a further statement about your awareness of that image.

There is no single look. The suit, as the "uniform" for a woman aspiring to a managerial position, is no longer an absolute rule. Guidelines about dress have become more flexible. "Presence" involves not only appearance but also self-confidence and knowledge.

A good haircut is essential. Short to medium-length hair is most appropriate for the woman seeking a professional position. Keep away from an "extreme" look. Your makeup should appear natural.

Whatever you do, make any changes well in advance of your interview. It is important that you feel comfortable with any "new look" so you won't be anxious on the day of the interview. Your nails should be medium length. Keep away from shades that are distracting. If you are accustomed to wearing fragrance, make sure it isn't heavy. Never wear anything that is overpowering. While a beautifully tailored suit is always appropriate, you can arrive for an interview in a coordinating jacket and skirt (complemented by a minimum of jewelry) and carrying a light briefcase; this would be a very acceptable look.

When choosing colors, keep to an understated, conservative look. A solid color, a muted tweed or plaid, or a subtle pinstripe is always in good taste. You want your next employer to remember *you,* not your outfit.

If you generally wear bright colors, you can retain your personal style by choosing a scarf or blouse in a shade you particularly enjoy. The blouse or sweater you select to go with your suit should be white, off-white, beige, or a color complementary to your suit. For example, a scarlet or crimson blouse can brighten up a gray suit and contribute to your appearance, especially if red is a color you enjoy wearing.

Generally, your hosiery should be neutral. Stay away from heavily textured or patterned hosiery. As for shoes, keep away from extreme high heels, sandals, and flat shoes.

Keep your jewelry simple. Wearing four rings won't help you here! The key is never use anything so startling or overbearing that it detracts from the overall impression you want to make. The key point to remember is that good dress won't get you a job—but sloppy dress can cost you one. Be aware that there is an unspoken "managerial" dress code for women. It is more tailored than feminine (no plunging necklines or sheer fabrics) and enhances a "power" look.

This emphasizes a woman's ability to perform on the job, rather than her femininity. Make sure you look like you are ready for the income level to which you aspire. Body language is also important. Straight posture says that you take pride in your appearance.

How to handle
stressful interview questions

The second key to becoming great at high-level interviewing is to handle whatever objections may come up—and to do it in a way that is comfortable for you. Many of us are more conscious of our liabilities than our strengths. When confronted with a liability, we may become defensive, argumentative, or worst of all, acquiescent.

As mentioned, when faced with objections, the tendency is to become defensive. However, no one sells anything to people while they are arguing with them. You need to have a valid answer when an objection is raised, but jumping to the answer may seem defensive. To avoid that trap you can use a simple process called ARTS. It can help you handle a problem question in a comfortable and effective manner. The letters stand for the following:

A—Acknowledge the objection
R—Redirect the person's concern
T—Test to be sure you've removed the concern
S—Use a story to make your point

Whenever someone raises an objection, the tension level rises. What you want to achieve in step one is to reduce the tension level.

A—Acknowledge the objection.

Here's an example: *"I can understand your concern. It is certainly something we should discuss, and I would like to address it directly for you."* Or... *"You're very perceptive, and you've raised an interesting point. It deserves some frank discussion, and I'd like to address it for you."* The phrases you might use are not so important. Instead, it's the feeling you impart. You haven't gotten flustered. You have acted in a friendly and reassuring way; it's clear that you feel secure about your abilities in the area under question.

R—Redirect their concern.

Going further, here is an example of redirecting the person's concern: *"What qualities are you looking for in an ideal candidate that prompted you to bring this up?"*

Let's say the interviewer raised the objection that your experience was in a different industry. Now, you can't do too much about the fact that your experience was in a different industry, but you probably can show that you are someone who contributes quickly, so that is where you want to direct the conversation.

For example, *"When you raise that question, I understand that you want to be sure the person you put in this job is someone who will contribute quickly. Isn't that it?"* The interviewer will reaffirm that you are indeed correct. As you can see, with just a little thought it is very easy to refocus the conversation toward the positive qualities that are really on the interviewer's mind.

T—Use a testing question to see if you removed their concern.

Here is an example of asking a testing question: *"If I could show that I could contribute quickly, even when it comes to learning a great deal of new information, would that help?"* After you get a positive response, you have the option of going directly to your answer, or you can introduce one of your key strengths. You might say: *"If I could show you that I work well under pressure, might that ease your concern somewhat?"*

S—Use a supporting story to confirm your point.

The final thing to do is to use a supporting story as part of your answer, ending it with a feedback question that will keep the conversation positive. Remember, what really counts is the fact that you did not get flustered. Instead, you had a friendly exchange in which you built positive feelings.

If you've done it right, interviewers won't be all that concerned about whether your answer is exactly correct. Instead, they'll be thinking, *"This person handled that situation very well."* Learn how to use this process, and for every concern, you should have your answer ready.

To recap, the second key to interviewing success rests with your ability to handle whatever objections may come up and to do it in a way that is comfortable for you. Get used to the simple process just outlined, and you will be amazed at how effective you will be.

14

Negotiation: Five Rules For Success

An awful lot of people are happy just to get an offer. But it's easy to do much more. Negotiation can be comfortable and predictable. The key is quite simple... be prepared and always follow these five negotiation rules. It's a straightforward process and works every time.

Negotiation—Rule #1
Always appear sincere and reasonable

In the job search situation, intimidation and attack strategies have no value. One-upmanship can cost you the job. Here you're setting the tone for your long-term relationship. In fact, most people don't like "negotiation" because they associate it with confrontation, being tough and role playing—something that does not come naturally. The best negotiators are very prepared but avoid anything that might cause irritation. Follow the best negotiators and make sure to be sincere and reasonable, never cold or calculating.

Negotiation—Rule #2
Avoid discussions about money

You need to avoid the lessons we see others learning every day. Here's an example. One client was a general manager with Exxon, earning a substantial income, but wanting to win a new job at a 15% increase. After two meetings, the CEO said, *"Bill, we'd like to have you join us, and I'd like to work out something attractive for you. What have you been used to earning at Exxon?"* At that point, having been encouraged, Bill explained his present income. To make a long story short, he accepted a position at a nice increase. However, he later found out that the last person had been paid 40% more, and that the company expected to match it. Now, the moral is simply that you should never negotiate based on where you've been. Negotiation is like poker. Don't lay your earnings on the table!

Premature discussions about money can be a deal breaker. Besides, the more enthusiastic an employer becomes, the more likely he'll be willing to pay more. Sometimes an interviewer will begin like this: "Jim, before we get started, I'd like to know how much money you are looking for." Here is a possible response.

"Charles, I could talk more intelligently about my circumstances after I know a bit more about the job and the contribution that's possible. Will this job have line responsibilities?" Or, *"Charles, I would not take your time if I did not have a fairly good idea of the range you could pay. If we can agree that my experience fits your needs, I doubt we'll have a problem on compensation."*

Once again, the U-turn strategy can help you here. Here's how it works: *"For my part, I am most interested in the situation and the people I will work with, the company and my role in the overall effort. And while money is important, I'm not locked into a specific figure, because of these considerations."*

Using this approach, you remain gracious and friendly while avoiding a direct answer. If an interviewer persists about how much you earned, here is one possible response: *"I would rather avoid discussing compensation until later on. Challenge is most important to me, and I would like to talk money after I know you want me for the job. Is that agreeable to you?"*

Negotiation—Rule #3
Express vulnerability and never demand

Let the firm know that accepting the job as offered would cause you difficulties. This plays to the employer's desire to make sure you are happy, so you can devote your full energies to the job. For example, you can be flattered by the offer, but say that you may have to sacrifice your lifestyle, and disappoint your family in order to afford the job:

"I love the job and really want to join with you, but we'd have difficulty making ends meet. Is there a chance you could go a little higher?"

Questioning, rather than demanding, is the rule. The best negotiators persuade others through questions. This gives them the information they need to put themselves in control. It also gives them time to think and never has them putting all their cards on the table.

Good negotiators will not say, "I do not agree with you because." Rather, they will say, "Charles, you do make a good point, but I wonder if there is room for another view." They would never say, "That would not be any good for me." Instead, they might say, "Charles, could you tell me how you think this would work for me?" Then they will follow up with questions, so the employer can discover that the proposal is not quite enough. And that is your goal: to let employers discover for themselves the validity of your request. If your questions lead them to discover they were wrong, they will be more disposed to changing the terms.

Negotiation—Rule #4
Never commit when you get an offer

When offered a job, praise the company and explain that you need some time to consider it. *"Charles, I am pleased you made me an offer. This is an outstanding firm, and the position has great promise. I am sure you can appreciate that I would like some time to give it further consideration. It would not present any problem, would it, if I were to get back to you tomorrow?"*

When you call back, after opening with one or two positive statements, consider raising the possibility of redefining the job. Your conversation might go something like this: *"Charles, with children entering college, I had done some planning based on an income that was $10,000 higher. Would it be possible to take another look at the job specs? For my part, I know that if you could make a modest additional investment, my performance will show you a handsome return. I sincerely hope that we can make some adjustment. Can we take a look at it?"*

Of course, if you do not want to redefine the job, but you would still like to raise the salary, you can use the same technique, but show vulnerability, then suggest that a dollar figure be added to the base. Normally, if that figure is within 15% of what you have been offered, the employer will not take offense and will grant you part of it. Of course, asking for more money is a negative, and needs to be balanced by positives. Here is an approach to consider:

"Charles, I cannot tell you how pleased I am. The challenge is there, and I think my experience is perfect for the job. There is one problem, however. You see, one of the main reasons I wanted to make a change was for financial balance. Can you see your way clear to adding $10,000 to the base? It would ease my family situation considerably."

Negotiation—Rule #5
Use your enthusiasm

If you load maximum enthusiasm into your statements, it becomes nearly impossible for the employer to conclude that you should not be with them. At the same time, follow the principle of introducing other criteria on which to base the offer. This can include the importance of the job to the firm, what you would make with a raise where you are, your total compensation package, what you believe the market is for your background, or other offers you are considering.

In the example that follows, notice how there are no demands, only questions. By your inviting employers to explore the situation with you, they are free to reach their own conclusions about whether their offer is too low. Using this approach, you come across as enthusiastic, sincere, and slightly vulnerable, never as cold, calculating, or aggressively demanding, or as someone who is putting them in a corner. Your comment might be:

"Charles, let me first tell you once again how pleased I am over the offer. I am very positive about the prospect of joining you. I've had the chance now to give it some more thought, and I can only say that my enthusiasm has continued to increase. This is the job I want. It's a situation where I could look forward to staying with the firm for the long-term. There is one hurdle that I have to overcome. You see, I've been underpaid for some time, and it has created a financial situation where I need to start earning at a rate which reflects my ability to contribute.

"If I stayed where I am, I'd be due for a raise, which would put me close to your offer. In talking with other firms, I've discovered that some of them realize this, and they have mentioned ranges that are 25% higher. Now, I don't want to work for those organizations—I want to work for you. But I do have some pressing financial needs. Perhaps the firm could approve a higher offer. Can we pursue this together?"

Now let's turn to what you should negotiate. Negotiating the nature of the job is your number one goal. Compensation is determined by the responsibilities of the job. So, reshape the job, and the salary range will be higher. For example:

"Charles, there is no doubt that this is a good job. However, based on what you have told me, I believe I could be even more helpful if a few related elements were added. There are three areas where my experience could make a big difference. I'd like to discuss them, so we can see if they could be included in the job description."

You might then go on to talk about the areas where the firm could capitalize on your experience. Believe it or not, reshaping the job can often be that simple. Can you see from the example how the principles were applied? The manner was positive and matter-of-fact, with no confrontation.

A reminder list—the things you might negotiate

❑ Base salary, commissions, and insurance. You might also try for a signing bonus.

❑ Profit-sharing and pension plans. If you negotiate a share of profits, know the accounting methods.

❑ Severance payments. A standard agreement covers a year's compensation, and is triggered if the firm lessens your responsibilities or tries to relocate you.

❑ Stock option purchase plans. If you purchase stock at market price, the company may buy shares under your name up to a percentage of your income.

❑ Stock grants. You will most likely be obligated for taxes based upon the market value of shares given.

❑ ISOs (incentive stock options). This is an option to purchase a certain number of shares at market value on a given day, generally exercisable some years away. The primary value of ISOs is that should you eventually buy them, no tax is due on the day you purchase the shares.

❑ Restricted stock units. These are pegged in value; e.g., as one share of stock for every five units. The key is when you can convert to cash or shares.

❑ Phantom stock options and stock appreciation rights. You receive the difference in value between the time granted and value when converted.

❑ Non-qualified stock options. An option to purchase stock below market prices. Tax will be due on the difference between the price at which you exercise your right of purchase and the market value of the stock purchased.

❑ Relocation expenses. E.g., house purchase, moving expenses, mortgage rate differential, real estate brokerage, closing costs, cost of bridge loan, trips to look for a home, lodging fees, tuition, installation of materials, and spouse reemployment services.

❑ Other perks can include automobile lease, luncheon, athletic or country club membership, child care, physical exam, disability pay, legal assistance, product discounts, dining room privileges, financial planning assistance, tuition reimbursement, CPA and tax assistance, short-term loans, insurance benefits after termination, special reimbursement for foreign service, outplacement assistance, and deferred compensation.

If you don't have any success in your negotiations, then shift from the "present" and focus instead on "futures," e.g. a review after six months, a better title, an automatic increase after time.

❑ Contracts. The following are usually incorporated: the length of the agreement, your specific assignment, your title, location, whom you report to, your compensation and what happens if there is a merger or if you are fired. It should also cover the specific items on the negotiation list that are part of your package. By the way, in most large firms, both signing bonuses and generous severance packages are spreading down the ladder. This is especially true when relocation is involved.

❑ Termination agreement. In most cases, agreements provide for a minimum of six months' salary, insurance, and outplacement.

15

Eight Things to do if You Lose Your Job

Three out of four people lose a job at least once during their careers, and the higher you go, the greater the risk. The good news is that virtually everyone becomes reemployed. You can do it quickly and successfully, while others would settle for much less than what they really deserve.

Today, unemployment is looked at from a far different perspective than in years past. For the most part, someone who becomes unemployed is viewed as a victim of economics beyond anyone's control.

Nevertheless, for those who lose their jobs, there can be a feeling of shock, disbelief, and even fear. It can mean the loss of many symbols of security that we take for granted. When we have a job, we have a place to go, an opportunity to achieve, and people to work with, including close friends. Even in those cases where people resign, their initial feelings of self-confidence can quickly give way to concern and doubt if they don't land a new job quickly. Obviously, loss of income can also cause great apprehension.

If you lose a job, there are eight steps to take right away

1. Start on your campaign immediately. Don't take a long vacation and don't retreat socially. Your advantage will be your ability to devote all of your time to job hunting. The best psychological boost you can get will come from having a schedule full of activity: breakfast meetings, lunches, interviews, letter writing, phone calls, and follow-ups. The way to do that is to get into action and give your job search top priority.

2. Get support from your employer. In addition to negotiating your outplacement assistance, the firm might even provide office space, secretarial help, and the use of a phone. You will also need to get total agreement on the reason for your separation. If there were negatives involved, work out an explanation that puts you in the best light. Look for clarification that the termination was due to factors beyond your control, such as a cutback, merger, or reorganization.

   By the way, never make the mistake of implying threats. If you are in a position to harm your employer, they will know about it without your saying so, and they'll be taking it into account in dealing with you.

3. Invest in your campaign right away. Ask for the type of outplacement assistance that will benefit you the most. If your firm refuses to provide help, you haven't lost anything. If they do, make sure you select the company, or ask to apply the funds they have allocated to the service of your choice.

4. Get access to an office phone. It helps to have a base of operations at an office. You might be able to use the number of a friend who can have his/her secretary take messages for you, or list a phone number under your own consulting service. At the very least, establish a work station in your home and let everyone know it is to be treated as your office.

5. Get yourself a friend who will be a source of encouragement and who can be a good sounding board. Share your progress and maintain communication with that person throughout the campaign.

6. Do a complete financial plan that assumes that you may be unemployed for quite a while. Allow sufficient funds to enable you to dress well, to get any professional help you need, and to actively pursue a job campaign.

7. Be as physically active as you can. Many people who have not been active have found that as more time passed, the less capable they were—psychologically and emotionally—to go out and do what must be done to win the right new job.

8. Don't be overanxious. Never beg for a position or try to explain your situation in print. Everyone likes to hire talent that is hard to find.

Handling liabilities

As important as your assets and skills are, you also need to be aware of anything that might be viewed as a shortcoming in the eyes of potential employers. Sometimes liabilities are overlooked. On other occasions they are mistakenly thought to be so serious that job hunters conclude that no corrective action can be taken.

To be successful, you should develop your strategy for handling any potential liability before you get involved in interviews. You know what your problem areas are. Give careful thought to how you should minimize their impact in all of your communications, both written and verbal.

By the way, some of the common liabilities that can cause a negative perception include: you're unemployed; you'll need to change industries; you've stayed too long with one employer; you're too old; you've changed jobs too often; you may be too generalized or too specialized; your career has peaked; your achievements aren't measurable; you lack experience in blue-chip firms; your jobs have been too similar; and your work history has gaps. Keep in mind that there is virtually no career problem that has not already been successfully resolved by someone else.

16

Building Your Will to Succeed

There is nothing that will be more critical to your career search success. Approach getting a new job as being inevitable. Your positive attitude is what can help you do it sooner rather than later.

A positive attitude is the single most common thread among all winners. It separates people from the tens of thousands who simply give up, settle for less, or remain in unattractive situations. It's easy to build a will to succeed if you're ready to work at it.

Now, it won't be news to you that if you truly believe in yourself, you will have the best possible chance of achieving the most you are capable of. So, it's a good time to remind yourself of all of the good things you have done, and what you can do in the future. This starts with looking at your past, with what psychologists have called "selective perception"; namely, concentrate on the positive things and ignore the negative. Your next step is to work on your beliefs. The idea here is to list positive things you "can do."

Your second step is to get rid of beliefs that might inhibit your will to succeed. Psychologists tell us that the beliefs we hold have a lot to do with the kind of world we experience. If, for example, you believe the economy is bad and firms are not hiring, you will go through the news and pay attention to items about layoffs or declines in sales.

Set your expectations
higher and put them to work

When many athletes are asked about their success, they often reply, "We expected all along that we would win." A look at leaders in almost any field also reveals a common theme. Whether it's a scientist, educator, salesperson, movie personality, or leader of industry, you'll find that all had very positive expectations of themselves.

Inspirational leaders tell us that it is possible to work on our expectations by visualizing good things happening. What we used to call daydreaming, experts now call "positive imaging."

Picture yourself achieving high goals, cutting costs, hiring others to work for you, bringing in new business and more. Whatever you choose for your positive visualizations, the important thing is to work on them every day. They will give you a new-found power and self-confidence. However, you also need to project some of those internal positives to the outside world. Start by talking to people about your positive expectations. This reaffirms your own commitment. You have put yourself on the line—you've let others know that you are committed to achieving your goals.

This, in turn, helps create the kind of environment where people make positive decisions about hiring. You'll have to work at this, but it's easy and it's fun. Good posture, a spring in your step, a firm handshake, a confident look in your eye, and comments which reveal a positive outlook can all help.

A brief review of self-esteem, stress, and the mind-body link

It's important to share with you a few observations about people who succeed beyond their expectations. Now in these situations there are two variables that help bring out unusual success. One of them is the ability to recognize and act on opportunities. The other has to do with the ability to overcome setbacks, and build self-esteem to levels that propel success.

Some people seem to possess a unique ability to constantly send themselves positive, healthy messages that add meaning to their lives. These people overcome fear of failure by coming to grips with themselves.

They build their self-esteem by acknowledging their mistakes, weaknesses, and downfalls. Rather than denying them, they discover positives and remind themselves of and take pride in even their smallest personal, social, or business triumphs. With successful people it isn't the size of the triumph that counts; these people recognize small victories and good things about themselves and keep them in the forefront of their minds.

When it comes to job hunting, the people who succeed through building self-esteem also seem to do so by creating some form of self-love, by liking what they are and the stage of life they are in, rather than wanting to be in someone else's shoes.

Time and time again, we have seen people succeed because they simply believed they could and others fail because they thought they couldn't. Once they've got their focus, certain people also seem to literally be able to "will" their success. Like competitors in any field, these people manage to psych themselves up and get into a routine that enables them to put forth amazing energy in pursuit of the right job.

This is especially important, because when you're coping with unusual stress, the mind can only dwell on one thing at a time, and you need to make it something good that enables you to be in action.

These people, the ones who achieve both unusual and unexpected success, also constantly motivate and remotivate themselves by setting goals, and by focusing on what they can control. They also turn their long-term job hunting goal into a *mini-series of short-term goals* so they can be succeeding along the way. Another similarity among these people is their ability to concentrate. Like top athletes who have a string of good performances, they seem to catch the flow. They clear their minds, ignoring anything that might otherwise distract them from achieving daily goals.

The last point I would like to make relating to these people has to do with feeling good physically. Certain people simply make themselves feel better. For example, people who may have been out of shape or in good shape, but who then vary or add to their routine by starting to run every day, or who start taking vitamins such as C, E, etc. Now, this is not written from scientific evidence, but whatever they do, within days I've seen people believing they are feeling better, sometimes after feeling down, and then translating that into other actions, which led to their ultimate success.

Make things happen by simply getting into action. Too many people make excuses for not getting into action. If, on the other hand, you look at the lives of achievers in any field, you will see that in addition to positive expectations, another common thread is they are very active people. Taking action is in itself like taking an energy tonic. When people get into action on anything, they no longer have time to worry about whether they will achieve their goal.

Private Marketing Campaigns
by Princeton/Masters

For better or worse, the term "outplacement" has come to mean any form of career assistance provided by employers who release staff—from career workshops through executive counseling. Traditional services, however, do not meet the needs of most job seekers.

Most outplacement firms act as "way-stations" for unemployed people—where counselors give advice, but where people are still left to do the real work of preparing and executing a campaign. Our approach is different. We play a proactive role, doing much of the work that's required and making a career search far more convenient. Essentially, we manage private marketing campaigns for each person we assist. Here's an overview of the three stages of our service.

Stage I:
We present a complete marketing plan on how each person should be marketed

We ask people to complete our *Career History and Marketability Profile*. This may be done at home. Completing it is a very personal experience, and it surfaces all the critical information we need. Then a team of our consultants analyzes their situation, accomplishments, and potential, and we put together a highly customized marketing plan. When we have the plan finalized, our staff presents it in a way similar to an ad agency presenting a campaign. Here's what is covered in a typical marketing plan presentation:

Marketable assets and solutions for liabilities

We usually uncover 20 or more strengths that each person has, which need to be described to the market. Also, if liabilities exist, we present corrective strategies, e.g. concerns about age, being unemployed, having too narrow or too broad a background, having been underpaid, etc. The strategies we agree upon are incorporated into all communications.

Uncovering career and industry options

We then present the moves that people might be able to make into new careers, frontier industries, and growth situations. All key industries and possible career paths are suggested. After we explain why each person may be right for each one, we zero in on finalized goals for the campaign.

An action plan for getting interviews

We then present a customized action plan for helping each of our clients get the right interviews. It covers precisely what a person should do, and how, when, and where.

An interviewing game plan
and negotiation strategies

This is to give people an edge in interviews, and help them control the pace and direction of each situation. Questions are anticipated and suggested answers developed. We also cover our ideas on what they should say or omit, and video training is available. The last part of our marketing plans involves preparing people to negotiate their best package.

To present everything in Stage I takes the better part of a day. At that point, each person we assist has the benefit of all of our analysis about how he or she can be marketed.

Stage II:
We provide professional writing and research to identify leads, contacts, and openings

Our next step is to present the resumes and letters that we have written for each client. Here we typically have developed the full series of biographies mentioned on pages 28 and 29. For each person we also professionally draft 10 to 12 different letters that might be required in the campaign.

We have also put together a unique research capability for coming up with leads, contacts, and openings for our clients—one that can often save weeks and months of time. As part of this, we have assembled the finest information files that current technology can provide. We use them to uncover the organizations and people who are high probability targets for responding to our clients' credentials.

The right employers to contact

From our files on over 10,000,000 private and public firms, we can develop a customized selection of employers and people for possible contact. This is based on any metropolitan area our clients prefer, the specific industries that interest them, the size of company they may wish to consider, and more.

The right high-tech firms to contact

Now most high tech firms are private, locally based, and hard to find. If clients are interested, we can also help them quickly zero in on firms that might be attractive career possibilities. One way this is done is from a remarkable file covering 35,000 of the most interesting high-tech firms.

Leads to growth companies

Our research department also tracks the country's fastest growing firms who are often seeking talent in many areas. Employers we follow were called growth companies by *Business Week*, *Forbes*, *Fortune*, *Financial Week*, or leading magazines or newspapers, or we learned that they were raising capital to expand.

Leads through venture capital firms

These firms supply capital to expanding organizations. From a special supplementary file, we can recommend companies and people to get in touch with here as well.

Names of appropriate recruiters to contact

From our recruiter file of over 7,000 firms, our staff can compile custom selections of recruiters who have the highest probability of being interested in your credentials.

Advertised openings from throughout the U.S.

To help people cover the market in a convenient way, we monitor executive openings as they appear in dozens of major papers, from *The New York Times* to *The San Diego Union*.

Employment leads to emerging opportunities

From over 450 business media, we can retrieve extracts from articles on growth situations, new divisions, new products, reorganizations, and acquisitions. These opportunities often indicate that unadvertised openings are available.

The Internet and other sources

Through our research we are able to direct our clients to a wide range of sources for finding information on possible leads and openings. Having a superior research capability *is not* something you can do on your own. Each year throughout our network, we spend over a million dollars in this area alone. However, when we share this cost among our thousands of clients, we bring them a capability that can dramatically enhance the speed of their campaigns.

> *Stage II can be completed with Stage I. An extra half day is required for presentation.*

Stage III:
We manage each campaign, and provide support every step of the way

Once a campaign is ready to launch, our work can involve managing mailings, providing new research for uncovering leads, contacts, and openings, as well as developing research on firms that express interest in our clients. We can be a sounding board to advise our clients on every opportunity that presents itself. Our philosophy here is simple. We work closely with our clients every step of the way, whether it be consulting, marketing, or research support, giving them every competitive advantage we can.

For more information

In our world of overnight deliveries, faxes, and advanced telecommunications, we can help people very quickly, regardless of their industry, career field, or location. If you or your company would like help in assisting executives, please give us a call.

In the domestic U.S.

For descriptive literature or more information, call Mark Austin or Pam Miller at 800-770-1170, or fax him/her your resume at 303-721-6617.

Outside of the U.S.

For descriptive literature or more information, call, write, or fax John Phillips at our corporate headquarters. Princeton/Masters International, 7951 E. Maplewood, Suite 333, Englewood, CO 80111. Call (303) 771-6100 or fax your resume or request to (303) 721-6617.